CONNECTING WITH A FRIEND

CONNECTING WITH A FRIEND

PAUL WELTER

Tyndale House
Publishers, Inc.
Wheaton, Illinois

ACKNOWLEDGMENTS

Many of my trainees in counseling and helping skills over the years have offered suggestions for improving the methods used. These trainees have included former students, workshop participants, college residence hall staff, retirement center personnel and residents, and nursing home staff and residents.

Dr. Marvin Knittel, who contributed one of the chapters, has been my partner in team-teaching the Counseling Skills course, a college class that develops many of the skills discussed here. Marv and I have worked together for sixteen years, and I have learned a great deal about teaching and counseling from him. He is an unusually effective teacher, counselor, psychologist, and psychodramatist.

A number of persons volunteered to have conversations with me about matters of concern to them, with the understanding that verbatims of the conversations would be used to illustrate various counseling skills. Their quest to heal and grow, and their permission to share the conversations, made the "live" presentations in this book possible. Names and some details were changed to assure anonymity.

Readers of major portions of the manuscript include Doug and Sue Frerichs, Marvin Knittel, Kent Estes, and Carl Malmgren. The suggestions of each of the readers resulted in a considerably leaner final draft of the manuscript. Lillian, my wife, read the various revisions of the manuscript and made a number of useful editorial suggestions. She was also my partner on the word processor in producing the drafts of the manuscript.

The Scripture quotations, unless otherwise noted, are from *The Bible in Today's English Version.* Copyright © American Bible Society, 1966, 1971, 1976.

First printing, November 1985
Library of Congress Catalog Card Number 85–51331
ISBN 0-8423–0426–6

CONTENTS

Preface   7
Introduction   9

PART ONE: FOCUSING ON THE FRIEND

1. Focusing on the Person Rather than the Topic   15
2. Overcoming Fears   27
3. Individualizing   43

PART TWO: SKILLS THAT DEEPEN THE CONVERSATIONAL FLOW

4. Understanding   51
5. Name That Tune—by Marvin Knittel   57
6. Timing   67
7. Effective Questioning   77

PART THREE: REBUILDING A SENSE OF WORTH

8. Affirming Unique Strengths   93
9. Helping with Tasks and Relationships   107

PART FOUR: TUNING IN TO THE SPIRITUAL DIMENSION

10. Using Our Weaknesses to Help Others   119
11. Using the Bible in Counseling   125
12. Utilizing Other Care-Givers   139
13. Using Metaphors and Telling Stories   145

PART FIVE: OVERCOMING RESISTANCE
14. Identifying and Removing Obstacles to Change   161
15. Challenging   173
16. Resolving and Mediating Conflicts   181

PART SIX: HEALING AND GROWTH IN SMALL GROUPS
17. Developing a Releasing Style of Group Leadership   195
18. Creating and Nourishing a Renewal-Support-Training Group   203

Appendix A: Suggested Readings   213
Appendix B: A Checklist for Preferred Learning Channels   217
Notes   219
Index   221

PREFACE

This is the third book of a series on helping. *How to Help a Friend,* the first in the series, teaches readers how to help others by approaching them through the avenues of life-styles and learning channels. The focus of the second book in the series, *Learning from Children,* is on *receiving* help. Children can help us find renewal and joy in our lives. They can also be our mentors, teaching us how to reach out to others in a more loving, effective way.

This present book, *Connecting with a Friend,* is meant to assist you in developing eighteen specific counseling skills. The book's main theme—freeing people—comes from the last three years of my life, during which I've worked hard—and played hard—at learning from children. Children are "released people" because they only know how to be what they are.

Jesus said, "If the Son sets you free, then you will be really free" (John 8:36). But many people, like Lazarus whom Jesus raised from the dead, are still bound by "graveclothes." We can have a ministry of releasing people, just as Jesus' followers did when he said to them, "Untie him, and let him go."

INTRODUCTION

I have been training professional counselors for twenty years. Unfortunately, there are not enough professional counselors to begin to meet the needs of all the people who are suffering emotionally. Also, many people refuse to see a counselor or psychologist. Therefore there is a need to train people to function, at times, as counselors to their friends and family members.

It had been my dream to develop a college course that would "give away" counseling skills and specific how-to-help methods to anyone who wanted to enroll, not just to persons preparing for a professional career in counseling. The Counseling Skills class, now in its fifth year at the college where I teach, is the realization of that dream. The several hundred people who have taken this course represent a variety of occupations:

Accountants
Bankers
Barbers
Bartenders
Cafeteria managers
Coaches
College residence hall assistants

Computer programmers
Cosmetologists
Health care administrators
Homemakers
Hospice workers
Intensive care nurses
Nursing home staff
Pastors
Pharmacists
Retirement center staff
School administrators
School nurses
Secretaries
Social workers
Teachers

The purpose of the class and this book is to help people acquire counseling skills to use in many different settings:

1. *Family*—If one of the parents or children has taken time to develop systematically his or her counseling skills, the rest of the family benefits because of the improved level of communication that results.

2. *Friends*—An immense amount of human suffering is done alone. Some of this suffering can be relieved, or at least endured, if more people have counseling skills.

3. *Work setting*—Many persons do counseling every day at work, often without the benefit of systematic training in counseling skills. Included among these "human service" workers are people in jobs such as many of those listed above.

4. *Organizations and volunteer groups*—For example, many churches are identifying members who have special gifts of listening, caring, or counseling. The churches provide special counseling training for these naturally gifted people, who are then available to do even more effective caring with both members and nonmembers.

5. *Residential settings*—The specific skill training described in this book has been done with approximately a thousand

staff members in three residential settings: college residence
halls, retirement centers, and nursing homes. A common
element in these settings is that the residents have been thrust
into "community" after a major dislocation in their own
personal lives. Having people around who are effective
listeners and responders can ease the adjustment and help
build a truly caring community.

THE COURSE AND THIS BOOK

This book comes out of my experience in teaching the
Counseling Skills classes and training helpers in workshops and
residential settings. For the most part, the eighteen specific
counseling skills described here are the same as those taught in
the course. The terms *counseling* and *helping* are used
interchangeably throughout this book to refer to those skills by
which we facilitate another's personal, social, or spiritual
development, including both healing and growth.

We use the List of Topics for Conversations shown in
chapter one to provide additional in-class practice. The class
size has increased to the point where we now team-teach it.
Dr. Marvin Knittel, who contributed chapter five, "Name That
Tune," is the other half of the team.

The course and workshop have provided a reality base for
this book. I know this method of acquiring counseling skills
works, since it has been field-tested over a period of years. I
hope you make it work for you.

One way to make it work is to help people move towards
wellness. There is an emphasis on wellness throughout the
pages that follow, and I believe what Bruce Larson says in
There's a Lot More to Health Than Not Being Sick:

*Jesus, the most incredible physician of all time, did not focus
on pathology. He did not make the healing of disease his
primary ministry. Over the three-year period of his ministry,
he healed literally thousands, but there seems to be no
indication that he ever went out of his way to look for anyone*

who was ill. His healing was incidental to his preaching and teaching ministry, to his encounters with people and his concern for their salvation or wholeness.[1]

The emphasis on wellness in the following pages is developed by focusing on ways to release people. It is not enough to help others get out of their immediate predicaments. They need to be released—set free—to respond to life in all its fullness.

Each of the eighteen chapters that follow is designed to help you develop a specific skill. I recommend that you study and apply one skill a week. Eighteen weeks is approximately the length of a college semester and will give you the same amount of time to work at these skills as the students have in our classes.

How to Help a Friend continues to be one of many useful resources available for helping others. Therefore, this present book is not meant to replace it, but rather to stand alongside it. I tried to avoid duplicating material. For example, crisis intervention is not covered in a specific chapter or section in this book, because much of the previous book was on this subject. On the other hand, several kinds of crises are dealt with here by using specific situations to illustrate the given skill under consideration.

There are several counseling skills that help us connect with another person. These skills need to be used early and effectively in any helping conversation, if we are to construct a bridge across the interpersonal space that will bear the heavy traffic of healing and growth.

These skills include:

Focusing on the Person Rather Than the Topic
Overcoming Fears
Individualizing

PART **1**

FOCUSING ON THE FRIEND

ONE

FOCUSING ON THE PERSON RATHER THAN THE TOPIC

If we could be convicted of felony for stealing conversations, how many of us would be behind bars? Since many of the conversations of our world are topic-centered, they provide a natural setting for such thievery. A friend says to me, "We had a great vacation in the mountains. They are really beautiful!" If I reply, "I really like the mountains, too. One of my favorite places is . . ." I am guilty of taking away the conversation from the other person. Such dialogue stealing is sometimes called "party talk," or "class-reunion conversation." In such exchanges, the two persons conversing watch each other carefully to see when there is a pause for breath, then jump in and pull the conversation back to themselves, using the *same topic* in an attempt to legitimize the theft. Both feel cheated when the conversation ends.

The skill of focusing on the person rather than the topic means that we leave the old method of topic-centered dialogue and substitute person-centered conversations, particularly when we wish to be helpful to another person. It is a kind thing to do to keep the focus on the person who initiates the discussion.

Francis of Assisi prayed that he might seek to understand

rather than to be understood. If two people are trying to be understood, there is no one left to try to understand. It is essential that one of the two people try to understand, while the other one is trying to be understood. Then the time will come when the roles will be reversed.

It is not easy to seek to understand rather than to be understood, as one person noted:

The difficulty I found with this skill, focusing on the person, is that maybe I am a little selfish. And also I found it hard to listen. I usually want to share what is going on with me, maybe more than I want to listen to someone else. This is a skill I definitely need to work on!

PHYSICAL CENTERING

The first step in focusing on the person is *physical centering*. The opposite of physical centering would be if, as you were talking to me, I pulled back, turned my body away from you, picked lint off my trousers, and looked out the window.

That's what it is not. Then what is it? It is when my body says, "I want very much to hear what you have to say to me." For a good model of physical centering, look at a person who is participating in a dramatic moment in a movie or TV program. This skill involves squaring your body toward the person whom you are listening to, using eye contact, and being within handshake distance. Each person has varying space needs, and everyone has ways to let you know if you are too close.

A twenty-five-year-old woman summarized what learning this new helping skill had done for her marriage:

I have learned that physical centering is powerful in that its use can deepen any conversation.... My husband, who was the target of my first conversations employing physical center-ing, knew when I was practicing this skill. Although I presently use physical centering in almost all our conversations, he now seems unaware of it. As a result of my working on this skill, we have a greater number of conversations than we previously did, and these talks have a much deeper content. In a way, physical centering has revolutionized our relationship!

Another person described how she began working to gain more skill in physical centering and focusing on the person:

I spent all week playing around with physical-centering skills. I wanted to see how they worked and how they didn't work. My first experience when I concentrated on physical centering was very successful. I faced her, leaned forward, and kept good eye contact. I used quite a few leading statements and open-ended questions. My experience was with one of my roommates. She's a hard person to get to know and doesn't share easily. She seemed very comfortable sharing with me. She talked for almost forty-five minutes.

Physical centering has different effects on different people, as the following man discovered:

I found physical centering worked well with some people but not with others. In a conversation with an acquaintance, maintaining eye contact seemed to make her uncomfortable. She kept looking away. In most of the conversations I had, however, people seemed to open up more when I looked directly at them and stayed at a fairly close distance.

Another person learned a tremendously important truth about the value of physical centering to the listener:

Whenever I talk to someone, I turn to them or face them, trying to keep eye contact. I also move closer or sit next to them. Physical centering helps me to really pay attention and listen.

This is a powerful idea—that the *listener* is able to concentrate more effectively by using physical centering. With these thoughts about the body, let's move ahead to focusing the conversation, the second step in focusing on the person.

CONVERSATION FOCUS

The woman mentioned earlier, who "spent all week playing around" with the skill of physical centering, also tried an experiment with focusing:

My second experience was a bit more involved. It was with a friend who really needed to talk. I decided I was going to listen to her, but every once in a while I was going to try listening without using these skills and see what happened.

When we started talking, my body was centered and my listening was focused on her. She shared intently and I listened for about twenty minutes. I wanted to get her going good before I tried my experiment. She was sharing an incident where she had been hurt by a guy. After she had talked for a while, I took a deep breath and dived in. "Yeah, that happened to me, too," I stated, and repeated an entire scenario of my own, similar to the one she had shared. She listened, but I could tell she was trying to cut in. I wouldn't let her. When I finished she was quiet for a minute and then she started where she had left off. We went back and forth like that for a while, then I started feeling guilty, so I focused on her again.

The person who did this experiment said that after she started listening again, the conversation came to an effective conclusion, with her friend's feeling "helped."

SUMMARY

This skill—focusing on the person rather than the topic—includes both physical centering and conversational focus. It is the first skill we need to develop for effective counseling, because it is the foundation for all the other helping skills. How do we practice this important skill so that we make it an effective part of our repertoire of helping skills? This is where The Built-In User's Manual for this book can be useful. The rest of this chapter is designed as a manual for practicing not only the skill discussed in this chapter, but also the other seventeen helping skills that follow. The Built-In User's Manual will help you make the transition from learning about a specific helping skill to actually putting that skill into practice and then improving it until it becomes a regular part of your helping interactions.

THE BUILT-IN USER'S MANUAL

If you have decided to broaden and deepen your helping skills in a systematic way, you may follow the built-in workbook approach described below. The steps outlined are the same ones we use in our Counseling Skills class. You may choose to work alone at this or with others—a class, staff members from the institution or agency in which you work, a church organization, or some other small group. Whether you work by yourself or with others, the following steps apply:

1. *Practice the skill in Life-Lab.* After you have finished reading a chapter, such as this one, on a specific skill, apply what you are learning in at least three actual conversations. How many conversations do you have each week? Whatever work you do, you probably have scores of verbal exchanges each day (home, work, phone), which would total into the hundreds each week. These conversations make up *Life-Lab.* All of life is a laboratory for practicing the skills taught in this book. You pay no fees to use this lab, and it need not take any extra time. It has the potential of benefiting you and the person with whom you are talking.

This can work for you if you *intentionally* use one of the skills in some of the conversations of your week. A helping skill such as "focusing on the person rather than the topic" is not a method to be used just in "counseling," but in all of life. Most of the skills presented in this book are applicable in everyday conversations.

Intentionally working on a given skill may seem artificial to you at first, but that is true of *any* skill. First it will seem wooden and uncomfortable; then increasingly natural and comfortable; and finally automatic and "forgotten." As you begin developing a skill, it is important to remember that just because it feels artificial does not mean it is phony. Irrigation is artificial, and it makes things grow!

2. *Use the List of Topics for Conversations.* Many of us have numerous conversations each day that have little meaning. Having a reference such as the List of Topics for Conversations shown here provides us with a way of nudging our talk from the weather to something that matters. Or this list can be used once in a while as the basis for family conversations. We can select our topic so it is not invasive, and we can choose to share at any level we wish. For example, each family member might have time to talk about a topic while waiting to be served at the pizza shop.

List of topics for conversations. Communicating with our family, friends, and fellow workers will mean more if we talk about things that matter. Here are some topics that are meaningful to many people. Most are clear enough, except perhaps Numbers 5 and 21. Sid Simon says that a "cookie person" is someone, usually in our early lives, who loved us unconditionally and invested time and attention in us. A "mentor" is someone we select as a one-to-one teacher to guide us in some specific area, for example, developing our tennis skills, learning Spanish, or growing spiritually.

1. A goal that's important to me is...
2. A personal quality or strength I cherish about myself is...
3. A predicament I'm facing is...
4. A memory that stands out is...
5. A cookie person in my early life was...
6. A joy in my life right now is...
7. A dream (quest) I would like to have come true someday is...
8. A regret I need to deal with is...

  9. A challenge before me is...
 10. A fear I would like to be free of is...
 11. My self-worth is...
 12. A relationship that means a lot to me is...
 13. A concern I have is...
 14. I would like to celebrate...
 15. One of my most important beliefs is...
 16. A thing (object) that has a lot of meaning is...
 17. An accomplishment that I feel good about is...
 18. A person to whom I need to say "I love you" is...
 19. My listening ability is...
 20. I find courage by...
 21. A mentor of mine (has been) is...
 22. A part of me that needs healing is...
 23. Something I need to change, but that I'm resisting chang-
     ing, is...
 24. I'm surprised that...
 25. A helping skill that I...
 26. My spiritual growth...
 27. The most creative thing I do is...
 28. I feel most renewed when...
 29. The first time I realized that God loved me just the way I
     am was...
 30. When I look at the future, I...

3. *Relive the conversation.* The first step in developing a skill
is to practice it. This can be done, as noted above, either by
using the skill in your regular conversations throughout the
week, or by introducing the List of Topics for Conversations
to friends or family members and then talking about one of
these topics. After the conversation, the next step is to *relive*
it. Those who work with psychodrama have a saying that we
cannot understand an experience in our lives until we have
lived through it twice. I am coming to believe that this principle is true. Therefore, the following methods of reliving the
conversations will be described: *feedback, journaling, personal*

reflection, and *reporting to a small group.* These are the same methods that we have asked members of our Counseling Skills class to use to relive their conversations. Another method is to audiotape or videotape the conversations, then listen to or view the tapes. But this method, although used in the training of professional counselors, has some disadvantages in most conversations. One of the biggest drawbacks is that it can intimidate the person with whom we are talking.

FEEDBACK. If you have a close relationship with the person to whom you have been talking, you may wish to tell him/her you are working to improve your conversational and helping skills and would like some feedback. You could ask how the conversation went, which of your responses were useful, and what suggestions the person has for your further improvement.

JOURNALING. By journaling, I mean writing an account of the conversation as soon as possible after it takes place. You include not only the primary interactions as you remember them, but also your reactions, feelings, and concerns as you recall them. Your journaling will consist of one or two paragraphs about each of your conversations. Some questions regarding the skill introduced in this chapter include: Were you able to maintain eye contact most of the time? What body posture did you use? How did the other person respond to your physical centering? Did you snatch the conversation focus back to yourself at any time?

If you keep your journaling brief, it will not become cumbersome. It is usually stimulating and will provide a "journey" experience as you read the entries again at the end of your work. You will be able to see how far you have come in the acquisition of important helping skills. Journaling will be especially useful to you if you are working on these skills alone. However, many people who work with a group have also found journaling helpful in recalling the conversation and reporting to the group.

There are some examples below of actual journal entries. The first one is about the skill of physical centering.

I found that I got much more out of a conversation when I used physical centering. I felt like the person talking to me was more comfortable and talked a greater length of time. I was more involved in the conversation, and it was more interesting to me. The other person seemed a bit intimidated by the eye contact, but was more relaxed by the end of the conversation. When I didn't use eye contact, the length of the conversation was considerably shorter and I felt like I was intruding on someone else's feelings. There wasn't that bond that seemed to develop when eye contact was used. The conversation was not very interesting, and I was rather relieved when it was over.

Another journal entry told how the helper had discovered a deeper, underlying concern in addition to the concern first mentioned:

My wife was talking about the difficulties we usually have getting our four-year-old to bed. I was able to focus on the fact that she was generally frustrated with child-rearing, her school-work, and her job. Although we didn't solve all the problems, just the fact that I could understand her frustration seemed to be of some help to her.

A third journal entry related how one person helped another get in touch with herself:

I had a conversation with a friend, dealing with the possibility of her husband getting laid off from his job. By centering physically and by keeping the conversation focus on her, I discovered her actions and her feelings were different. On the outside she was trying to act strong and had an attitude that "if the bills don't get paid, big deal! The bill collectors can't take away what I don't have." But inside there was fear as to whether there would even be food on the table and clothes on the kids' backs.

The above three journal entries illustrate how the journaling process helps to relive a conversation. Another way to do this is by reflecting.

PERSONAL REFLECTION. Most of us use this process unintentionally. By being intentional about it, we can enhance its value. It is much like journaling, except that nothing is written. We relive what happened as best we can, by thinking about it—about what happened and also about what did not happen. Unless one is quite disciplined and has excellent powers of concentration, this mode of reliving is not as thorough and accurate as it is with journaling. But if you are working solo to gain these skills and do not choose to use a journal, it does provide you with a way to relive the conversation. You may find that personal reflection is enhanced by talking your thoughts into a cassette recorder. This process sharpens the detail, makes the reliving more interesting, and provides a record to check back on later.

REPORTING TO A SMALL GROUP. A training group offers many advantages in acquiring helping skills. There is a sense of accountability that a group gives to its members. Because we know we will be reporting to the group, we remember to be intentional about our conversations. It is a good experience to have a safe place to tell about our successes and failures. A group often provides the necessary support and encouragement for continued learning.

A group can also help you "process" your conversations. Different members will provide you with new ways of viewing what happened as you report to them. Let's suppose you are part of a group of resident assistants in a college residence hall or a singles church group. If you form groups of two or three people, the reporting can be done fairly rapidly, and then you can do further work by re-forming into a large group and discussing the skill under consideration.

4. *Credit yourself.* To develop counseling or helping skills, we need to note what we do right. Otherwise, we may stop doing something that is working. Take time to mark your journal, mentally underline in your personal reflection, listen to what group members are affirming about your skills, and

write down several things you are doing that should become a permanent part of your helping approach.

5. *Target any necessary changes.* Are there words, mannerisms, or behaviors you need to drop or unlearn? Are there new questions or approaches you need to add to the specific skill you are developing? Target these changes by making a brief list and referring to this list from time to time.

The above steps comprise "The Built-in User's Manual" and will be referred to and augmented with each specific skill. It is hoped that one or more of the methods from this cafeteria of options will be attractive and useful to you.

Improving our focusing skills will help us connect with a friend. However, these skills will not be enough to make a vital connection possible if the other person is fearful. Therefore, the next skill that needs to be developed is that of overcoming fear.

TWO

OVERCOMING FEARS

When Marvin Knittel and I teach the Counseling Skills class, we demonstrate each of the specific skills. One of us will ask for a student volunteer who is willing to talk about one of the thirty topics from the List of Topics for Conversations in chapter one. Our students have rated these demonstrations as being very helpful in their learning. We use the demonstrations to show *a* way of utilizing a specific skill, not *the* way.

Because of the value of demonstrations in our course, I have included a number of actual conversations in this book. Therefore, to illustrate Skill 2, "Overcoming Fears," as well as some of the other skills that follow, I use actual verbatim quotes of conversations. There were more who volunteered to talk about a topic of their choice than I needed for purposes of illustration. I have found that people want to talk about things that matter to them if they can be assured they will be listened to. The students gave permission for all or any parts of the conversations to be used in this way. Some details are changed in the verbatims to assure anonymity.

You will notice "PW" doing the talking in every other response. That's me. My belief is that I need to be willing to risk laying out my actual responses if I am to have credibility in the training of counselors. And it is risky. There are a number of responses I would like to change. A few of my responses remind me of Samuel Johnson's reply concerning a question about one of the definitions in his dictionary: "A lady once asked him how he came to define Pastern as the knee of a horse: instead of making an elaborate defence [sic], as she expected, he at once answered, 'Ignorance, Madam, pure ignorance.' "[1]

A margin column is used to explain the reasons for many of the responses, and to show how a given response reflects the specific skill being studied.

Brad, a man in his mid-thirties, wanted to talk about Number 10 on the List of Topics for Conservations—*A fear I would like to be free of is. . . .*

PW1: Can you tell something about the fear you would like to be free of?

B1: Yeah, uh, I've felt this before, you know, in working with people. I guess I feel it right now, right at this very moment, and to me maybe I fear that I don't have anything to offer. . . . I don't want this to be a complete waste of your time and mine. . . . Also, I am working with kids in my church right now, and one of my fears is that I don't really have that much to teach them. But I've been talking with other people who have told me they really feel that I do, and people have sought me out.

B1: An encouraging sign here is that Brad has an awareness of his feelings at the moment. He is able to take his "emotional pulse." He is in touch with his fear.

PW2: You've found that others believe in you more than you do yourself?

PW2: Brad is experiencing a fear that he lacks teaching ability, despite assurance from others that he is able. I chose to respond by highlighting these contrasting views of himself.

B2: Yeah, that could be, I guess.... I'm especially looking at—not just a class deal where you sit down for one session and talk—but it will be a process that will take place over the next two or three years, possibly, with some of the kids on a one-to-one basis to help them grow in their relationship with Christ.

PW3: This fear you have, this feeling about yourself, are there areas of your life where you really don't have that?

PW3: The purpose of this response was to help Brad target more closely the areas of his life where he was afraid and where he was not.

B3: I'm an action person, so when I go to do something, I don't really have too many doubts as to how it will turn out. I just go do it. I think in an area of discipleship or counseling, that's when I wonder if I have that much to offer.... It may possibly stem somewhat from my education; I don't feel qualified....

PW4: A worry that since you don't have a college academic background, that this would keep you from being effective?

B4: Well, you know, maybe that's a crutch for me, kind of like our pastor said, "Jesus called some fishermen and made, you know, apostles out of them and then they went on and discipled people without any problem, and helped people."

PW5: A number of things I notice about you, Brad—first, a genuineness: you are yourself. That seems a very important first requirement for a helper. The second thing I notice about you is that you seem open to growth, and personal growth is really important to you.

PW5: Affirmation needs to be given fairly often, from my point of view. Someone said that affirmations are to be inhaled, not swallowed. I think this is a good point. It is not that an affirmation is not to be believed. It is rather that, like oxygen, we need a lot of it to live and grow.

B5: It really is. The growth hasn't always been there and, you know, I was finally brought to a place where growth could take place....

PW6: I think that's a third dimension of your life that I feel strongly—the spiritual dimension of your life. There's a deep flow there and that's a very important dimension of your life, and the rest of your life forms around that.

B6: Yeah, it really does, I guess. I really do feel like that is what my life is centered around.... *[Pause]*

PW7: The fear of not being able to have enough to give is getting in your way and sounds like something you really want to deal with.

PW7: Brad's pause seemed like a good opportunity to get back to his fear of being inadequate.

B7: I don't know for sure how I can overcome that other than to just believe that I do have something, and go ahead and enter into those relationships, praying that God would use me.

PW8: I think what you are talking about has risk in it.

PW8: At this point, when the fear had been targeted, I wanted to introduce the element of risking and courage.

B8: Yeah, yeah, there is an element of risk.

PW9: What would be the worst thing that could happen? Like maybe in our session if you felt that somehow you weren't useful, what is the deepest part of the fear that you face?

PW9: This response was to help Brad move from his fear in connection with himself as a teacher or leader of a small group to a present fear that he was facing. He had mentioned "this very moment" in his first statement, but I had chosen to respond at that point to a more general lack of self-confidence.

B9: I think the rejection. Somebody saying, "I'm not really getting enough out of this; I'm going to go elsewhere."

B9: The question that was asked in PW9 elicited the center of what Brad was facing and trying to deal with—the stark, nagging fear of abandonment, and particularly of rejection—that is, abandonment with cause.

PW10: Like—if in this session— somehow I might reject you?

B10: Yeah, and say, "We're not getting enough out of this," or something like that. Or that I'll be spending time with some of the kids at church, and they'll say, "I'm not getting what I was looking for, so I think I'll go look somewhere else."

PW11: In terms of the fact that your spiritual life is very important to you, do you have any kind of that feeling with God? Or is it just with people that you would be rejected?

PW11: A fear of abandonment or rejection by God is sometimes triggered by the actual or perceived rejection of a very close person, and I wanted Brad to get at his feeling about God in this respect.

B11: I think just with people.... I think maybe I used to have that feeling with God somewhat. I looked at God like I looked at my dad, and my dad was unloving and strict and I think showed probably a lot of rejection to me, and I carried that over, of course, in my dealings with God when I was a young Christian.

B11: Brad indicates here that he had done some important previous thinking, connecting his early view of his father with his early view of God.

[At this point Brad told how he had been working recently to improve his relationship with his father.]

PW12: In your growing-up days you were having to strive all the time to avoid rejection from your dad.

B12: Yeah. The love part was pretty much nonexistent.... He took care of us, he furnished us a house and food and stuff like that, but as far as a father-son relationship or anything like that, that was almost nonexistent. The feelings of rejection started when I was about eight or nine or ten and carried right through.... And then I guess I took an indepen-

B12: Brad distinguishes here in a very clear, aware way the difference between providing for the physical needs of family, and building relationships. He also draws a connection from this to the self-imposed alienation of his growing-up days.

dent attitude that I didn't need any-body. But anytime anybody would do anything, then I would feel that re-jection, and think, well, I don't need you anyway—which was hard.

PW13: You found yourself continuing to follow that pattern?

PW13: This is an example of a transitioning re-sponse from one time zone to another. I was interested in helping Brad move from the past up towards the present.

B13: Uh-huh, following that same pattern with my family. I've really mellowed over the years, but I can look back and see how, especially with our first child, I was ending up doing some of the very same things. Some of the little nit-picking things that really didn't mean anything any-way, you know, like eating every-thing on your plate. It was ridiculous, but a person can take that and really carry it to an extreme to where it's almost unbearable for the child, and I found myself doing things almost like that.

PW14: You went through at some point a time of growing awareness that you were becoming pretty nega-tive. You were planning not to be-come like your father, but you saw yourself becoming like that. And it sounds like also in your childhood you went through a period of a lot of pain, but somehow maybe you didn't

PW14: At this point I wanted to introduce the concepts of pain and anger. I knocked on this door, not knowing whether or not Brad would open it.

feel the pain so much as the anger. So that you began to rebel.

B14: Well, I ended up rebelling a whole lot.

PW15: Then you came to the place where you were able to let go of that. How did you do that? I don't sense bitterness in you.

PW15. Letting go requires a great deal of courage. I wanted to help Brad explore how he let go of the bitterness and to credit himself with that.

B15: No. I guess it didn't just happen overnight that I became aware. I was struggling at the same time with my relationship with God. Just like my relationship with my father, it was also hard for me to talk with him. I didn't feel like I could trust him because, like my dad or other people that I was with, God could probably let me down. As far as being bitter with my dad or anything like that, I think I took care of that. I didn't go up to my dad and tell him that I did not have any bitter feelings or anything like that, but I just prayerfully turned all that over to God and told God how I felt that I would like to overcome the bitterness, overcome the hurt and rejection, and I'd like to just turn that over to him, and that I didn't want to be bitter. I forgave my dad for the things he had done. You know, he was probably doing a lot of things that he did because of the way that he was raised. I guess I finally came to think about that and to real-

B15: Christians have the resource of forgiveness available to them. I found from my own experience of trying to help persons let the past go, that Christians have a distinct plus at this point.

ize that he may have been acting towards his family just like I was reacting to my family—the way I was raised.

PW16: And so you've been able to break the chain?

PW16: Parents have the opportunity to break the chain, that is, to parent in a different way than they were parented. I wanted to credit Brad with doing just that.

B16: Yeah, our relationship is a lot better.

B16: Brad, in responses B13, B16, and B17, traces how growing up with a feeling of rejection can lead people, when they become parents, to reject a number of inconsequential things that their children do and thus convey a feeling of rejection to them as persons.

PW17: Well, with God, as you think about your relationship with your dad and then God, does God now seem a person to you who loves you unconditionally?

B17: Uh-huh, yeah. He sure does. I'm finally freed up to where I can show love and express warmth to my children. Before, I thought they might reject me, and because I didn't want to be rejected or feel the hurt, I didn't express a lot of love or warmth or take any. You know, I was taking care of them physically and all this but not really showing them the love. . . .

PW18: Do you have some unfinished business with your father? Even though you have forgiven him, it sounds like there's something there, if you could find a way that you would like to finish or do something with. Or is that right?

PW18: Because of the fact that Brad had said earlier that he forgave his father without talking with him, I wanted to check to see if Brad, at this point, had the courage to go directly to his father, or if he saw the timing as not being appropriate.

B18: I don't know. . . .

PW19: Even approaching that with your father might not be an easy thing.

B18, 19, 20: The task of going to his father looms much too large at this time for Brad to choose to do it. I decided only to open the issue rather than press it.

B19: No, it wouldn't.

PW20: Because your father's not open to that?

B20: You know, maybe, as our relationship grows, maybe there will come a time when maybe we'll be able to sit down and think back, and maybe he'll feel open enough to say, "Well, this is what caused it." *[Pause]*

PW21: You mentioned a very important term a while ago, the term "freed-up," and I was thinking of it in terms of fear, that as you became less afraid you find yourself more free, more free to love your children, more free to just be you, express warmth; that's exciting.

PW21: The concept of being released or freed-up is so powerful that I typically try to underscore it or reinforce it when it is mentioned.

B21: Yeah, I think that's probably right, because I'm beginning to realize that it's not that my kids are trying to reject me; they are just doing

B21: The story that Brad tells here is a very powerful one. It was a turning point in Brad's behavior with his own children. He

what they want to do. It's me that's feeling rejected and sometimes I have to deal with that.... One little incident, when you look back it seems utterly insignificant, but I was really feeling rejected for probably a half a day or so, until I just dealt with it and thought through what had taken place.

It had snowed the night before, so when I got up I went out and started scooping snow, kinda expecting that the children would probably be out in a little while to help. Well, sure enough, here they came outside, got their snow shovels, but instead of helping me, they ran over to the neighbors and started doing the neighbors' walks! Now, why? And that just started to gnaw on me a little, you know, and pretty soon I was thinking they could not help their poor old dad out here scooping snow, but they would run over to the neighbors and help. Then it just kinda dawned on me, well, we're always telling them to be looking for jobs and work where they can earn some money for themselves, and to do some jobs for other people, and here I am feeling rejected when they decided to go out and do just that. Then I had to think through that and think what they did was all right, and it wasn't that big of a deal for me to scoop off the sidewalks and the drives, and by my thinking

discovers, as he's out scooping snow and feeling abused and sorry for himself, how it is to look at a situation from his children's point of view. Parents who do not go through this particular line of reasoning may abuse their children. If the parent feels rejected by the child and feels abused, it is not a long step to reacting in a violent way to the child.

This story, plus the additional information that Brad has learned how to apologize to his children, says a great deal for his personal growth and openness to new insights.

I believe that his telling this story to someone who cared brought additional insight and determination to Brad. Sometimes the most important thing we can do for friends is to listen to their stories.

through and overcoming my rejection, I had less anger toward them.

Another thing I've started to do is something my dad never did and that's to apologize to them. And sometimes I'll apologize to them for being angry, hoping that will help our relationship and not let them feel rejection like I did.

PW22: You are working hard to accept them. And part of your own journey is accepting yourself because you did feel rejection in your early years. And that journey has not been an easy one for you.

B22: No.

PW23: Are there any other thoughts you have been having about what we've been working on tonight?

B23: I guess the only thing I wanted to say and didn't is that the process of overcoming rejection will probably take me the rest of my life, but just seeing progress is good.

B23: I was excited at this point to hear Brad give himself credit for making progress in his battle against the fear of rejection. This conversation shows that Brad is finding courage to face life more freed from the immobilizing fear of abandonment and rejection.

COURAGE

Courage is the virtue that enabled Brad to connect with himself and with me in this conversation. To connect with another person in a significant dialogue, we need to be able to release such courage in the other person and in ourselves.

Courage allows us to risk in a relationship. With this virtue we announce to ourselves and to the world that we choose *life!* Charlie Brown, Charles Schultz's cartoon creation, is a world-class example of resilience and courage. Although it was Charlie Brown's point of view that when he came onto the stage of life, there was no part written for him, he has responded with courage. Every time he falls down, he gets up again, dusts himself off, and chooses life. His baseball team suffers humiliating defeats, but Charlie finds courage to play again and even anticipates a winning season.

Courage is extremely important as a virtue because it allows us to function when fear is present. Insight alone is never sufficient to bring us to action when we are afraid. Chances are, we have known for a long time what we need to do, but fear is immobilizing us. A first-grader helped me understand how to function despite the presence of fear. When I asked him what *brave* meant, he said, "It's when you are scared to death but do it anyway." How do people overcome fear? Some seem to do it by *desensitization*, a process of overcoming fear a little bit at a time. One person was so afraid of snakes that she would not turn the page of a book on which there was a picture of one. To overcome this phobia, she needed to work a step at a time with increasing intensities of the fear until finally she was able to go walking in a meadow.

In other situations, people may choose to walk straight into their greatest fear. We may need to go directly to the person we most dread to confront and "have it out." A middle-aged woman chose to go to her father and talk about the incestuous relationship he had made her a part of decades earlier. Both were very shaken, but that courageous step was one she believed she needed to take to help bring about healing.

How do we find courage? It comes through encouragement, which usually comes from the presence of a stronger person. Think of a person you know who is out of courage and to some degree immobilized by fear. A first step is to get to know that person well enough so that you have some insight about what would be encouraging to him/her. The same act can encourage one person and discourage another. One person will respond to a challenge, and another will back off from the same challenge. Encouragement is like medicine—it needs to be individually prescribed. I worked to encourage Brad in the above session by affirming (PW5, 6) and by crediting (PW15, 16, 18, 22).

SENSE OF ADVENTURE

An adventure usually implies new experiences. It also suggests a journey, and this is usually a shared journey with the potential of danger. There is an element of quest present. There may be a sense of exhilaration. The use of some of these words can help one overcome fear. They imply that life is a process and that part of that process is a struggle against adversity. Some of these "process" terms that appear in the conversation above include:

Flow (PW6)
The deepest part of the fear? (PW9)
Growing-up days (PW12)
Continuing (PW13)
Growing awareness (PW14)
Able to break the chain (PW16)
Unfinished business (PW18)
Journey (PW22)

LOVE DRIVES OUT FEAR

In addition to overcoming fear by encouragement and by appealing to the sense of adventure, a third way is to draw on the unlimited resources of love. One way I did this in the conversation with Brad was to mention the unconditional love of God (PW17). Conditional love is one of the greatest sources of fear, particularly with those like Brad who experience such love or have experienced it in the past. Many may actually have been loved unconditionally, but another kind of love was communicated. The message that came across was "I love you *if [when, because, sometimes,* etc.]," rather than "I love you." You—as a friend, a listener, a helper—can connect with others by communicating unconditional love and by referring to Jesus, the unconditional lover.

LIFE-LAB

How are you doing with your fears? Number 10 on the List of Topics for Conversations is *A fear I would like to be free of is.* . . . I suggest you share the list with a friend or two, and that you each discuss this topic, with the focus first on one of you, then on the other.

And as you practice your skills this week in helping others identify and overcome their fears, use the steps described in the Built-in User's Manual in chapter one to relive your conversations and improve your skills. Remember to work on Skill 1, "Focusing on the Person Rather Than the Topic," as well as Skill 2, "Overcoming Fear." Each week, practice the previous skills as well as the current skill you are studying.

THREE

INDIVIDUALIZING

Two proud relatives look at the new infant. "Look at the way Char's nose curves up. Doesn't she look just like her mother!" The other adult looks from a different angle and says, "Notice the shape of her face. I think she's the image of her sister Doris!"

Twelve or thirteen years later, on a Monday in late August or early September, this same child, now equipped with an almost adult body and the panic that most seventh-graders feel on their first day at junior high school, hesitantly steps into her first-period class and takes a seat. Her teacher, who has been at the school many years, calls the roll. As Char responds to her name, he looks at her a second time. Sometime during the first week of school he asks her, "Did you have an older sister named Doris?" And then he says, "She was an excellent student." Char, who already knew this, walks out of the room at the end of the period—once again in the shadow of her sister.

Her relatives and her teacher were both doing what comes naturally—comparing. It's fun to look for a family resemblance in a baby's face, and teachers like to recall superior students. However, every person is incomparable—incapable of being compared. The only things we can compare are noses, faces, grades, ages, weights, and that sort of thing. And it usually does not work to try to connect with someone on the basis of his/her similarities to another person. In fact, this is often a barrier to connecting. We stand our best chance if we connect with a unique quality, not a reminder of a shared characteristic. That unique quality may be a special interest, ability, joy, or quest.

When I read the Gospels, I am moved by the way Jesus connected with people by individualizing. Even his stories reveal this concern for the identity of each person.

The man who goes in through the gate is the shepherd of the sheep. The gatekeeper opens the gate for him; the sheep hear his voice as he calls his own sheep by name, and he leads them out. (John 10:2, 3)

One of the meanings of this story excerpt to me is that we will leave a safe place and risk "going out" with one who consistently cares for us and calls us by name—sees us as an individual.

Carl Jung wrote about the need to individualize. He noted that we gain *knowledge* about people by regarding them scientifically as comparative units, but that we gain *understanding* of an individual by seeing that person's uniqueness. He put it in an interesting way:

Hence it is not the universal and the regular that characterize the individual, but rather the unique. He is not to be understood as a recurrent unit but as something unique and singular which in the last analysis can neither be known nor compared with anything else. . . . If I want to understand an individual human being, I must lay aside all scientific knowledge of the average man and discard all theories in order to adopt a completely new and unprejudiced attitude.[1]

MAKING THE CONNECTION THROUGH INDIVIDUALIZING

Our little dog, Dexter, died recently. He was part miniature poodle and part terrier, and his light brown, silky hair came

down over his eyes. I once saw a drawing of two such dogs
on a greeting card with the caption, "I wish we could see
more of each other!" I grieved over Dexter's death, so I
talked to a number of people about it during the week that
followed. Four of the first five people I talked with said something like, "I remember when our dog died, I...." These
were caring people with the best of intentions. I say they
were well-intentioned because they were not trying to steal
the conversation, but were trying to connect with my grief by
comparing it to one they had experienced. But I did not feel
cared for—because their responses were missing the target.

These people missed a connection with me because they
were not individualizing. They were comparing. But each
grief is incomparable. I wanted to say, "You will never understand my grief by bringing your own back to life. Listen to me
and try to understand what is unique in all the world about
my grief." I do not mean that my grief was more important
than theirs or anyone else's, but rather that it was different.

Suppose one of your parents has died some time ago. Then
your second parent dies. And you are now grieving not only
over the loss of a parent but also over being orphaned. One
can be orphaned at twenty or forty, just as one can be orphaned at four. And the loss of a second parent often carries
this added dimension of grief. But should I say to you, "I
know the emptiness and sadness that comes in a special way
with the death of a second parent, because I, too, have experienced that"? No! I know only about *my* grief, not about
yours. And the only way I can learn about your grief is by
listening intently to you.

I kept bringing up Dexter's death with people I knew, and
the fifth person I talked to listened to my grief. That person's
response was something like "You must have loved Dexter a
great deal." And thus, released, I began to talk about Dexter. I
spoke of his gentleness and what I had learned from observing this quality in him. I talked about the fun we had together. And I told of the special care he needed because of
his epilepsy. My friend just listened, asking questions now

and then or responding in other ways to keep the flow going. At the end of our conversation I felt cared for and understood. That one conversation moved me through a major portion of my grief and into almost a sense of celebration of Dexter's life. An amazing achievement! One person somehow knew not to focus inward on a past, similar grief, but to focus outward, to individualize, and thereby discover another person's unique grief.

Does this mean, then, that going through the "same" grief that another has gone through is not useful in understanding that person—that it can, in fact, get in the way? That is possible. However, it is more often an advantage in understanding that person, because we have experienced a deep sadness or sorrow and we are thus able to "weep with those who weep" (Romans 12:15b). If we have not experienced that level of grief, or if we have not worked through our own grief, we may try to "cheer up" the other person or "explain" the event that caused the grief. Both these attempts to help usually leave our friend worse off than we found him or her.

Individualizing is the opposite of narcissism. M. Scott Peck in his helpful book, *The Road Less Traveled*, discusses narcissism under the general heading "Love Is Separateness."

In its most extreme form the failure to perceive the separateness of the other is called narcissism. Frankly narcissistic individuals are actually unable to perceive their children, spouses or friends as being separate from themselves on an emotional level. [2]

Probably most of us would not be called narcissistic, but we may have some of that characteristic present. We focus on our own deep emotions and mistakenly think we thus understand what these emotions mean and feel like to our friends and family, as this college student noted:

Have you ever heard of getting hand-me-down clothes or toys from another family member or friend? If you have, that is great because now you will have an idea what I am talking about when I mention hand-me-down problems. If my older sister had a problem, she talked to Mom, and Mom had a solution for her. Then when I became old enough to have problems and go talk to Mom, she always told me, "Becky has had that kind of problem. I'll just switch names to yours." That didn't really start bothering me until I realized I couldn't have a unique problem or a problem all my own. Someone had always had it before me. Mom never neglected to help me, but I always knew that she had already solved a problem like that and she would have the solution.

Individualizing is a difficult task. What are some specific ways to improve this skill?

STEPS TO INDIVIDUALIZING

1. *Review the ideas in chapter one, "Focusing on the Person."* We often pull the conversation back to ourselves when we focus on the topic instead of the person. Concentrating on the other person frees us to begin the process of seeing the other person as unique in all the world. That process is individualizing.

2. *Resist the impulse to bring your own experience in as the "norm."* You will connect with the other person not by comparing normative experiences, but by understanding what is unique and individual in your friend's experience.

3. *Monitor your friend closely with your eyes and ears.* You will thus gather important information that will aid in individualizing. Moreover, this sensory concentration on another person will help keep your mind from flashing to your own experiences.

4. *Express your love by words, touch, eyes, and in other ways.* The expression of love forms a bond or connection when nothing else does. And, after all, individualizing is simply one way of expressing love.

LIFE-LAB
Remember, in your Life-Lab conversations this week, that the persons you talk with are as unique as their fingerprints. Look for and celebrate the qualities that make each person special.

After we have connected with another person, we can use several other specific skills to keep the helping process flowing and deepening. These process skills, which are at the core of all effective counseling, include:

Understanding
Name That Tune
Timing
Effective Questioning

PART 2

USING SKILLS THAT DEEPEN THE CONVERSATIONAL FLOW

FOUR

UNDERSTANDING

There is a special moment of awareness when we have understood someone. One person told about this moment:

This style of listening has been one of the most valuable techniques I have learned. I'm a person that just sees the outer shell of many people and I don't take the time to really see their feelings and viewpoints. But now I sometimes find myself waking up to a new world of understanding.

When we deeply understand another person, it is indeed a "waking up" experience. We have gotten outside ourselves; we have loved. It is this awareness of loving and being loved that often brings tears to the eyes of both the one being understood and the one doing the understanding. When someone understands us, it is as if we become willing to break out of our shell.

The Chick and the Shell

It's comfortable
   Safe,
      Cozy,
         Warm,
   Keeping me alive.

But it's also boring.
   Dark,
     Cramped,
     Lonely,
And keeping me from living.
   Do I want out?
     Part of me does.
Sometimes I think I'm ready.
   I hear noises from out there.
     And my shell is thin;
   I can see some light coming in.
   But I'm scared.
Some of the noises are unfriendly.
   And my shell is thin.
How do I bring myself to destroy
   What has always protected me?
     I need warmth to get ready
     For such a violent act.

Being understood can provide the warmth that enables us to break out of our own shells.

Diane, the woman in the following conversation, wanted to talk about Number 9 on the List of Topics for Conversations— *A challenge before me is. . . .* Her husband's job was going to require them to move in a few months. She did not want to give up her own job. And to make matters worse, they did not know where her husband's next assignment would be.

D1: Neither one of us has ever lived in a family where we moved. We grew up in the same house, and our parents still live in the same house, so this moving is kind of a frighten-ing thing. We have a child now who is two, and so it hit me the other night that he's never going to know this house that he was born in and lived in; he will never remember that. So the sadness is starting to—the grief process, I guess, is starting.

PW1: You're grieving for your child's future—he doesn't feel it yet but it's a grief you feel like he'll have sometime.

PW1: Diane's first response revealed two deep emotions—fear and grief. I chose to respond to the latter because it seemed to me at the time to be the deeper one.

D2: Well, I'm afraid he will. I guess other kids adapt to it because that's all they've ever known.... I'm not unhappy about leaving where we live. I haven't gotten a lot of close friends there and I feel like I don't have any role models.... When we were in college we had good friends and we went and visited them, and it was just wonderful to be with them, and that's what I'm missing. I have a hunger for that kind of friendship and acceptance, just the way I am.

D2: Diane moves rapidly in her second response to her own grief—the loss of close friends.

PW2: Just the way you are—where you can be you.

D3: Uh-huh, and I don't have to worry about the way people think. I kinda hold back and that's probably why I don't have any friends, because nobody really knows me because I never show my true self, and what I did show them wasn't very exciting—a busy little person. I worked full time and was home very seldom.

D3: In this response she identifies her shell, which is fear—the fear of self-disclosure. If we do not disclose our true selves, we never know whether or not we are loved. We only know how people respond to the self we do show—in Diane's case one that "wasn't very exciting—a busy little person." Her friends did not have the opportunity to respond to the real Diane, one who was sensitive and wanting to grow.

PW3: In order to be you, you need to have some sign of unconditional love or some indication it isn't just the role—you're you.

PW3: I tried with this response to convey my understanding of the deep need expressed in D2 and D3. I don't know whether or not it was effective.

D4: I want somebody that I can have some basic agreements on, and then we can discuss those. You can build on a point and go from there and grow. I think that I haven't grown in the five years I've been here, and I'm regretting it.

PW4: I sense a lot of underlying pain and hurting in terms of loneliness and in terms of a lack of personal growth.

PW4: All of Diane's previous responses, plus the "regretting" in D4, caused me to respond as I did here.

D5: Oh, yeah—and I feel guilty about that, too, because I think, well, this town has things to offer and I should have been able to do these things, or I could have grown in this area, so I feel guilty about hurting about it, see, and yet I really do hurt, you're right. . . .

PW5: As you try to think about the center of where you hurt, the pain that you have. . . can you identify that?

PW5: The work of "centering" is very important, whether it is with pain or some other emotion. I try to help people with this process. It almost always deepens the flow of the conversation.

D6: Well, I think when you were talking about loneliness earlier, that's where the tears welled up...and I don't know why I have to put some of my worth on what other people think, but I do. If I don't have friends, I don't have someone to share with, I think there's something wrong with me, and my self-image right now is the pits. I need someone right now to say, "You're fine. We like you just the way you are." Because I can't say that right now to myself, so that may be it! I want some people out there that I can relate to, that I can share with and be accepted by.

Diane went on from this point to discuss how her lack of self-esteem was leading to an impatience with her little boy. We then talked about ways for her to get in better control of herself at these times.

LIFE-LAB

There is a yearning in people to be understood. Therefore, when we have understood someone at a deep level, we need to convey that understanding. In the next chapter, Marvin Knittel explains a special way to understand people and then to let them know we have understood them. The name he gives to this process is an apt one—"Name That Tune." I recommend that you read Marv's chapter now. Then, after you have studied both chapters, put them into practice. The two chapters are complementary. This chapter is about understanding another person. Marv's chapter explains how to communicate that understanding to the other person. After reading Marv's chapter, give yourself two weeks to practice these important skills.

If you wish to study additional resources concerning these and other helping skills discussed in this book, you will find some described in Appendix A: Suggested Readings.

FIVE

NAME THAT TUNE

The yearning in people to be understood, which is the focus of the preceding chapter, is universal. But to be understood means that someone must be able to understand. And to understand someone means we need to hear what that person is saying about his or her life. That is not always as simple as it seems. Most of the time our conversations revolve around a description of the *events* in our lives. One person talks while the other waits for his or her turn. Usually, neither takes the effort to "hear" the other person. Neither feels really understood, because neither person hears the *personal message* that the events reflect.

Hearing and understanding the other person both require the ability to translate words into a theme. For example, Tommy, a third-grader, came home from school and described in detail how he ended up being the last person to be chosen for his soccer team during recess. His mother said, "I'll bet you felt hurt and disappointed." She was "naming a tune" she was hearing during the entire detailed description of the day. Not only did she name that tune (hurt and disappointment), but she was able to name it early on and thereby show true understanding all the while he was talking. Tommy felt the relief of knowing his mother understood. He also learned that feelings are important to share.

When no one seems to care about naming the tune—understanding—people sometimes stop trying to be understood. I have counseled with couples who have become so convinced that the other did not or could not understand that they turned their backs to one another—to guard the delicate shell that protected themselves, as Paul so vividly explains in his poem in the previous chapter.

HEAR WHAT I'M *NOT* SAYING

Perhaps these couples mentioned above were saying to one another, "Hear what I'm *not* saying!" Frequently, the most important things that we want others to understand are the unsaid things that are implied in what we say. Complex emotions may not lend themselves to easy descriptions with precise language. Our true feelings are often disguised—camouflaged not only from others but from ourselves. Sharing our feelings with someone who is devoted to understanding (naming that tune) helps to clarify our own feelings. I can recall having counseled with individuals experiencing personal pain and loneliness who were only able to show anger. When I was able to hear that pain—hear what the person was *not* saying—and communicate my understanding, the individual developed a greater self-understanding.

Another way to describe this sometimes perplexing human condition is to say that to truly understand another you must listen for the "un-words." Only by listening to these "un-words" can we accurately "name that tune." I have known young children as well as teenagers who kept an entire family in constant turmoil by their misbehavior, in a desperate effort to communicate a need to be needed and cared about. In effect, these young people were saying, "Please try to understand me. Please listen closely to what I'm *not* saying and name the tune I'm playing."

As Paul listened to Diane, he clearly was listening to the "un-words" so that he could name the tune. When Paul said,

"I sense a lot of underlying pain and hurting in terms of loneliness and in terms of personal growth," he was naming the tune. It was very important for Diane to hear Paul name her tune, which was being heard only indistinctly and as background noise to her.

PIPED-IN MUSIC

The background noise of which we are only vaguely aware at times is something like the piped-in music played in a supermarket. The music is always playing, but our need to concentrate on our shopping pushes the music below the surface of our awareness. The need to decide what is important in our lives from moment to moment occupies the forefront of our attention. However, the tune that may be relatively constant in our lives continues to play in the background, frequently affecting and often controlling our moods and emotions. We can go on for long periods of time, keeping busy coping with life and only fleetingly aware of the tune that plays the haunting chords of our own despair and loneliness. There are also people so desperately afraid to hear their own tune that they deliberately keep on the move doing one thing and then another, never willing to risk being idle or alone, because then they must listen to the confusing and sometimes frightening notes.

TWO KEYS UNLOCK THE DOOR

Safe-deposit boxes are a nonmusical image of the role of the counselor. We know that access to the contents of the box requires two keys—our own and one other. When the two keys are simultaneously inserted into the door of the safe-deposit box, it will open and the contents can be explored. Herein lies the mystery of how one person helps another. When *two* people work together, the possibility of opening that door and exploring the inner contents increases by geometric proportions. By hearing my own tune expressed by another, I can identify more easily the rhythm and the key in which it is written. It is of even greater assistance to me if I have a friend who is perceptive enough to be able to help me name the tune in only a few notes.

Here is an example from a journal entry of a student in our class:

Helen called Thursday morning and asked if she could return a book that she had borrowed. I said, "Of course, and plan on having coffee with me."

Over coffee she began telling me she couldn't stay long as she had to take cookies to school for her daughter's class birthday party. She began talking about how busy she was with her two girls, and that she had given up most of her social activities because she didn't have the time.

I said, "That must be very frustrating for you at times."

She smiled and said, "Oh, it's not so bad really, and I enjoy it most of the time. It's just that I never seem to have any time for me. I am room mother, den mother, and I pick up and deliver kids almost every day."

I said, "I get the feeling that even though you are smiling as you talk, you are feeling very put upon and resentful."

She said, "You just put your finger on it. I feel like running away some days with so many demands on me."

She talked for a while and said, "Mary, as I sit here talking to you, I realize that I've made myself into a slave. It is going to stop as of today. Some of the other mothers, working or not, can start taking some of the responsibility for driving and picking up. I'm going to call each one today. Now why didn't I think of this before!"

It can be seen that the main tune playing in the background was resentment. The interesting aspect of naming the tune with someone is that when he/she hears it "played back," it sounds more clear and sometimes different from when it is just background noise.

COMMON PITFALLS

Confusing your tune with someone else's. Sometimes the tune
we hear from someone else is *so* close to the tune playing
within us that the two become confused. It is possible to
name our own tune, when in fact it's the wrong one. The
result can be confusion. One student wrote the following in
his journal after explaining that he thought he knew his
friend well enough to know the tune she was playing: "But I
realized that I was naming the tune according to my ear and,
although the chords were close, I was naming an E-flat and
the real tune was the E chord."

Once the student focused on the tune his *friend* was playing, she was able to hear the words to her tune and gain
some insight that had not been there before. The student
wrote in his journal that the friend told him that she "had
never really put this tune into words before." The final entry
in his journal was: "...my friend and I are twice as close
since the correct naming of the tune."

It is interesting to observe that when two people discover
the basic tune that is being played, a greater and more meaningful level of intimacy results. The level of true understanding that goes on between two people is enhanced and the
opportunity to be truly human with one another increases.

The old familiar tune. Another pitfall is trying to fit the tune
you hear to a tune you have heard before—perhaps from
someone else. Although people are much more alike than
different, each of us is unique. Even though we may all experience a common emotion such as anger or joy, the experience is still unique because of all that each of us brings to
the experience. The composition of feelings and emotions for
each of us is as different as fingerprints.

Jan had just discontinued a close relationship with a young
man. I listened to her story and concluded that Jan was angry
and hurt. Jan corrected me and said she was simply disappointed they had not dropped the relationship before. I had

tried to equate Jan's tune with one I had heard many other times. I was wrong. I had not listened well enough to the uniqueness of Jan's story.

Hearing the story but not the message. When we listen and try to hear the tune of the other person, we often get caught up in the story details rather than the message. The tune is the message that the person is sending about him or herself. The story and all the details are simply the notes. Just as in any composition, the tune is discovered only when all of the notes are heard in some meaningful relationship to each other. A theme emerges not by adding one note to another but by hearing the notes in a meaningful pattern. For example, our national anthem is not "heard" if the notes are not played in proper sequence, timing, and rhythm. Therefore, as I have indicated before, listen for the "un-words" to discover the tune that continues to play in the background as your friend tells his/her story. Naming the tune that is constantly in the background is the essential ingredient in understanding and being understood.

Failing to listen for the "secondary tune." More than one tune can play at the same time, although one is usually playing more loudly than the others. When our daughter was married, the tune my wife, Donna, and I were most aware of was joy and celebration, especially the day of the wedding. Directly below that surface melody was yet another that was much more mellow and nostalgic. It was the tune of letting go and recognizing the "rite of passage." The primary theme of celebration could momentarily be interrupted by the secondary tune only when our thoughts would shift or someone would focus conversation in that direction. The point I am making is that we often must listen for more than one tune, because the tune below the surface is frequently very significant.

COMMON TUNES

There are some common tunes I have heard over and over in my counseling experience. Everyone seems to have his/her own unique arrangement, but the theme remains relatively constant. Here are a few tunes that seem to repeat themselves.

"I Only Want to Count." This tune is played by all groups. It is the tune being played by a wife in the kitchen, when she slams shut the cupboard door a little more vigorously than usual because her husband is sitting in the other room, reading the paper and seemingly oblivious to her needs. Her actions are clearly playing "I Only Want to Count." It is also the tune played by the child or the teenager who constantly pushes to get attention by keeping you busy and in his/her service.

There are a variety of arrangements to this tune. It can be played just as clearly by the person fearful of venturing outside of his/her shell as by someone who is loud, boisterous, and overbearing. Both are searching for some confirmation that they have value.

"Love Me for Me." That is a tune I frequently hear played by junior and senior high school students who are high achievers in academic as well as nonacademic areas. The first line of that tune seems to ask, "Am I loved for what I *do* or for what I *am?*" This is the dilemma that high achievers continue to face and that pushes them further into a feeling of loneliness and occasional depression. It is almost a self-fulfilling prophecy. The more the students achieve, the more praise they get for achieving, which in turn motivates them to achieve more—for which they receive more praise for achieving, and so on. Occasionally, a young man or woman deliberately fails in order to test the love of "significant others." At that moment the tune "Love Me for Me" becomes amplified beyond reasonable proportion.

"I'm Confused by Your Kind of Love." This is one of the tunes I frequently hear being played by incest victims. Over the past years I have worked with scores of young women who have been victims of incest and sexual abuse. Frequently, the perpetrator of the abuse has been a father or stepfather. The girl is perplexed because on the one hand she wants very much the love of the parent, while at the same time she feels powerless and guilty. She is left with the confusion that intimacy and sexuality are synonymous. So, the tune "I'm Confused by Your Kind of Love" seems to be played over and over again by the victims of sexual abuse.

"I'll Swallow My Feelings." There are many tunes that are played by individuals who have such relatively complex eating disorders as anorexia nervosa and bulimia. One often-played tune conveys the message that feelings need to be guarded or denied. Consequently, the feelings are internalized. In other words, the feelings are swallowed by the person with all the distaste and psychological indigestion that one would expect. Improvement is frequently observed when the individual with the eating disorder acknowledges the legitimacy of his/her feelings, assigns those feelings and emotions appropriate value, and ultimately decides what to own and not to own. A balanced diet of experiences and feelings frequently leads to a change in the tune.

"Please Fence Me In." Whenever I work with families, I am impressed by the precision with which children communicate this tune to their parents. I frequently am equally impressed by the difficulty the parents have in hearing the tune. The children essentially are saying, "Care enough to say no and give me boundaries." This tune is somewhat of a paradox. The theme of this book is helping people find freedom, and this tune appears to say, "Take away my freedom." The truth is that clear boundaries do give children freedom, because they know what the rules are. They become more released to exercise their individuality within those clearly established

limits. Once I heard a young child virtually describe in exact detail what he wanted his parents to do regarding the rules that he wanted to live by. The rules as he expressed them were reasonable and far more confining than what already existed. Paradoxically, the parents were not hearing "Please Fence Me In," but rather, "Don't Fence Me In."

LIFE-LAB

There are many, many more common tunes that could be related. The important first step is to be able to name the tune and, together with the other person, discover ways to respond to the tune or perhaps even change it.

I noted in beginning this chapter that we have a yearning to be understood. In the true sense of the word, that means knowing that someone else is looking at your world through your eyes and also hears the rhythm of your soul. To "name that tune" is to move beyond the silence, the surface music, and the dissonance, and dance with your friend to the most deeply felt melody he/she is playing. As a student wrote, "There is almost a mystical feeling when you recognize what that tune is!"

SIX

TIMING

Rhythm is a fundamental characteristic of life even before birth. The unborn baby senses the rhythm of the heartbeat and peristalsis of the mother. After the baby is born, there is a rhythm of nursing, sleeping, and waking. Later the child experiences the rhythms of night and day, the seasons, and the wind. There are the rhythmic patterns of infancy, child-hood, youth, middle age, and aging. Each person thus acquires an individual rate, a unique rhythm.

No other element in helping requires more sensitivity than timing, a technique by which we adjust our helping method and approach to the rhythm of the person with whom we are interacting. Most people tend to help at their own rate and their own rhythm. This usually results in their not being as useful as they otherwise would be.

I use the approach shown in Figure A as a way to honor the rhythm of the person with whom I am working. We usually encounter persons needing help when they are in a state of inaction. They need to be taking some kind of action, but they are not doing it. Often this immobilization is caused by their spending their energy brooding about their emotionally troubled state—for example, feeling depressed about feeling depressed.

THE PATHWAY TO ACTION

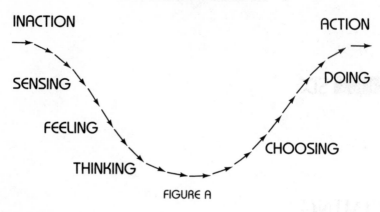

FIGURE A

THE DEEP VALLEY

You will notice that the drawing is in the shape of a deep valley. There are many crises in life that can lead us through such a valley. The one I will use here to illustrate the concept of timing occurs when a marriage partner chooses to have an affair. An affair results in an immense amount of human suffering—for the spouse or spouses involved, the children, the extended family, friends, and the participants themselves.

I remember one couple who sat facing me. Both were crying, suffering from a wrenching emotional pain, an ache so large and intense that they firmly believed it would never go away. He told of the affair he had begun and was trying to end. She told of the shock, of the terrible feelings of being rejected as a wife, a woman, a person. And she voiced her conviction that their marriage was now shattered.

What can family members, friends, and the Christian community do to help a couple rebuild their marriage after an affair? In some cases, nothing. If the person having the affair chooses to continue it, divorce usually results. If the offended mate opts for divorce and will not reconsider, nothing can be done. But, in many situations, something else can happen.

In an affair, the couple needs those around them to intervene. Their marriage needs to be placed by others in "intensive care," because those who are critically ill have difficulty acting for themselves. But who assigns a desperately ill marriage to intensive care? If anyone does, it will probably be those who are in a caring relationship with one or both mates and who have the courage to intervene. And the first step in intervention can be simply to express caring. The "deep valley" diagram shows a path or sequence a helper can take in staying with troubled persons, such as the couple above, as they move back to functioning again.

Visualize a troubled person or persons on the left side of the valley. People in that place are usually partially immobilized by their pain. They are neither working well nor loving well. They are so caught up in their own suffering that they are not meeting the needs of their tasks or their relationships. They are in a state of inaction. Most persons cannot simply jump across the chasm, going from inaction to action in one movement. But friends can accompany them down into the valley and through it. And the Lord has promised to be with us in the deepest valley of all (Psalm 23).

THE PATHWAY TO ACTION
The sequence shown below does not always work. Neither do all these steps always occur, nor in this order. But these five checkpoints have usually served as a trustworthy guide to me as I try to help a friend move toward action.

SENSING. People who are suffering are often unaware of much that is going on around them. Their vision is constricted—looking only for a way out of their pain. Their physical senses need to begin operating again. Friends can help here. It usually takes reactivating the senses to bring people back into the world outside of their own suffering. Go for a walk. Take them to lunch. Listen to some music. Smell a rose. Drink some coffee, tea, a soft drink, or even water. Work with the senses until you know you are in contact— you are communicating.

I once went with a friend to be with someone he knew

who had told him in a phone call, "I don't think I can make it through the night." She was so depressed that she would neither look up at us nor talk. I played a very sad song on her stereo while we made some coffee. We touched her. In a few minutes we had helped her begin to "come to her senses"—hearing, taste, smell (the aroma of the coffee), and touch. Later that evening she used her sense of sight when she began to look up and talk with us.

I believe she had been close to overdosing. When people "come to their senses," they are less likely to panic. Incidentally, the sad song was to communicate understanding. She looked me up later and said she knew by my choice of song that I understood how desperate she was.

FEELING. Let's go back to the feelings of the husband and wife mentioned above. I can help best by "being with" the couple in their pain without trying to make them feel better. The Bible is explicit in this regard: "Be happy with those who are happy, weep with those who weep" (Romans 12:15). There is a time for weeping. To try to make people feel better when they are suffering is to make light of their pain. An alternative to saying, "You shouldn't feel that way," a statement that violates Jesus' command not to judge others, is to be silent, to touch or hug the one who is suffering, or to say something like, "I want you to know I sense some of the pain you are going through right now." By listening accurately, accepting the expressed hurt and anger, and showing love, we can sometimes assist a couple to get to the place where both can think more clearly—where their minds are not as befuddled by pain as before.

THINKING. When husband and wife have expressed their hurting to a friend and to each other and feel understood, they are ready to move to the next place in their journey through their valley, a place where their thinking is clearer. They are still headed downward in their travels, but they are now prepared to gain new insights. Because of this openness, we can respond with reasoning and questioning. We can help them avoid impulsive actions by getting them to slow down and think through their next step.

Notice the importance of timing. If—in our first contact with persons who are in emotional pain—we try to reason with them, we are usually unsuccessful. First we have to "bring them to their senses," and then stay with them as they work through their feelings. Only then can we begin to reason with them. For example, when this husband and wife are thinking clearly, they are better able to understand how Christian forgiveness and mercy apply in their situation. At this point they would probably profit from reading J. Allan Petersen's excellent book regarding affairs, *The Myth of the Greener Grass.*[1]

CHOOSING. I find that I'm now often able to sense when people walk with great courage through the deepest part of their valley and start to look up. It is at this point that they begin to *choose life again.* For people undergoing deep emotional trauma, this is an absolutely critical juncture. Having made the most important choice of all—to live again—they can now make other decisions.

Now it is appropriate to ask the question, "What is your plan?" or "What do you see as your next step?" In terms of timing, this is the only point at which I could ask this question. It would not have been understood nor responded to earlier in the rhythm of helping. But now they are ready to begin choosing, not in a panicked state but in a considered way. At this point I may gently confront and question their values. As a Christian and as a friend, I have the obligation to *reprove*—"to call attention to the remissness of, usually with a kindly intent to correct or assist"—when necessary. If a person is planning to continue in the affair, I say to him/her, "What you are planning will cause more intense suffering to those you love, including yourself, than you can imagine." Pointing out the consequences of an action is usually more effective than telling the person not to do it. There is within most of us enough general cantankerousness and original sin to want to do what someone tells us not to.

The time of choosing is a time of looking at options, of

being challenged, and of visualizing consequences. A friend can be of great help at this stage. Left alone, many of us make choices that are difficult to live with tomorrow or next year.

DOING. Once the choices have been made, the "doing" begins. Many couples, like the one above, choose to get help from a counselor, or to spend "prime time" with each other every day, getting better acquainted and rebuilding their marriage. Some are fortunate in having a group of concerned Christians in their church or community to love and accept them—and to hold them accountable for their decisions. A number of couples who have rebuilt their marriages have told me they could not have made it if a group of friends had not kept on expressing their love and acceptance. Some have said they did not deserve this acceptance, and that was why the caring was so redemptive for them.

The couple referred to above has now come through the deep valley with the help of their friends. They have moved from a state of inaction to action. They, and their relationship, are still fragile and will need continued healing and growth, but the worst is probably behind them.

Sometimes people go directly from inaction to action in order to avoid having to deal with their pain. But it does not work well that way, because sooner or later the hurt will come out. We cannot carry the world on our shoulders, although each of us tries it at one time or another. We all know people who, instead of facing their predicaments, turn to everything from burying themselves in their work to numbing themselves with alcohol or other drugs. And so many times all they need is someone to listen and to talk with—to help them through that period. I think that is what timing is all about—knowing when and how to help others at the moment of their need. It is useful here to know the level of the urgency of their needs. My earlier book, *How to Help a Friend,* has a chart that describes the different need levels and shows how to discover at which level a person is functioning.

The five-column chart shown on the next page is to help you determine your strengths in the areas mentioned above.[2] Simply go down each column, checking those items that are typically true of you. Then tally the number of check marks in each column. Add the checks in all five columns, divide by five, and you will thus obtain an "average." If the checks in any column total two or three above the average, this indicates a strength. The checklist is not a scientific instrument, but it may give you some clues. If you are strong in the *sensing* area, you will probably be effective in connecting rapidly with the person experiencing emotional trauma. If you are strong in the *emotions* channel, you will be especially useful in helping your friend work through feelings. If you are strong in the *thinking* channel, you can help your friend analyze the situation and visualize the consequences. If *choosing* is your forte, you can serve as a model in this process. And if *action* is your strong point, you will emphasize by your life how to spend energy on getting things done rather than brooding about them.

A word of caution may be needed here. Many people tend to help by drawing only upon their own strong channel. Those who are great in the feeling channel may begin and end their helping here. And this is not enough. A person who is good at "thinking things through" may wonder why his/her friend (who is still caught up in his pain) is so "unreasonable" and "won't talk sense." In fact, entire schools or theories of helping and counseling have been started by people who emphasized the particular response style in which they themselves excelled.

Instead of using only the channel in which you excel, another approach is to utilize the strong channel of the person you are trying to help. For example, you may be a very logical person who thinks analytically. Your friend may be a very sensory person. If you begin by appealing to your friend's reason, you may miss altogether. Try getting in touch, using some of the methods mentioned above in the "sensing" paragraphs. You first have to go where a person is (needing sen-

RESPONDING-STYLE CHECKLIST

I. SENSES	II. EMOTIONS	III. THOUGHTS	IV. CHOICES	V. ACTIONS
1. You usually take time to eat slowly and to taste your food.	1. Someone has told you in the last six months that he/she appreciates your warmth.	1. You usually consider consequences before acting.	1. You make important decisions easily and decisively, rather than spend a lot of time worrying about them.	1. You generally live in the present by forgetting the past and not worrying about the future.
2. You like to have people touch you.	2. You usually are able to express angry feelings.	2. You usually plan purchases well in advance and resist buying on impulse.	2. You prefer to make your own decisions.	2. You are involved in life and rarely spend time "feeling miserable."
3. You usually concentrate carefully on what others tell you.	3. It is natural and easy for you to maintain eye contact with a person to whom you are talking.	3. You are prompt for appointments.	3. You usually have a clear sense of what is right and wrong.	3. You typically find it easy to sleep at night.
4. You listen to music for all the nuances, not just the melody.	4. You enjoy receiving compliments and react graciously.	4. You can visualize the results of your actions easily.	4. Life has a great deal of meaning for you.	4. Overall, you feel confident about your future.
5. You find it easy to touch people, especially those who are psychologically close to you.	5. You've been angry at someone in the last few weeks.	5. You usually plan ahead and avoid predicaments.	5. You have clear-cut personal goals.	5. You see yourself as a competent person.
6. You enjoy the fragrance of food.	6. You've told someone within the last week that you appreciate, like, or love him/her.	6. When you have a task to do, you typically do it rather than avoid it.	6. You can usually find the courage to make the decisions you need to.	6. You usually feel healthy and full of energy.
7. You literally take time to smell the flowers.	7. Others see you as a friendly person, easy to get to know.	7. You would classify yourself as dependable rather than undependable.	7. Right now you're finding it fairly easy to decide which of these areas you're strong in.	7. It is easy to concentrate on what you are reading.
8. You listen to others' voice inflections and variations to catch deeper meanings.	8. You smile as much or more than most people.	8. It seems to be easier for you than for most to stay within a budget.	8. You could quickly and easily list three or four values in life that are very important to you.	8. You usually finish what you start.
9. You "listen with your eyes," i.e., you observe facial movements and gestures of others to catch deeper meanings.	9. You rarely use sarcasm.	9. At a restaurant you rarely order more than you can eat.	9. Courage ranks high in your value system.	9. You enjoy beginning the day.
10. You are able effectively to "tune out" background sounds and listen accurately to the person who is talking.	10. You often share your deep feelings with others.	10. You find it easy to think through your day tomorrow.	10. You feel confident of your decision-making ability.	10. You view difficult circumstances as challenges rather than insurmountable obstacles.

sory experiences) to get him/her to join you where you are (needing to approach the predicament in a reasonable way).

LIFE-LAB

Up to this point, as we worked to acquire new counseling skills, we could almost be guaranteed the opportunity to apply our new skill in several conversations during the week. Now we cannot be so sure that this will happen. For example, not everyone (fortunately) is working through a crisis that requires a careful sense of timing in a conversation. How then do we approach Life-Lab from this point on in the book? I suggest you still work to apply the skill being studied, in at least three conversations each week. For example, this week, listen with your eyes to see those whose body language says they need an understanding ear.

Also, as you keep using the skills you have already developed, such as focusing on the person rather than the topic, many conversations will naturally proceed from a surface level to a much deeper flow of communication. Your alert use of timing will help release this flow.

SEVEN

EFFECTIVE QUESTIONING

Let's suppose you are in the midst of a predicament or emotional trauma, and you begin to talk with me about your situation. I will listen, then respond with statements and some questions. There are two totally different lines of questions I could use with you. The first would be designed to give me enough information so that I could analyze your situation and give you suggestions or advice concerning what to do about it. This is the method of interrogation. Its major disadvantage is that it shifts some of the responsibility for your life from your shoulders to mine. I am not suggesting that we should never ask questions to obtain information, but I think there is usually a better approach.

A second manner of questioning uses questions designed to help you find your own way. This leaves the responsibility with you. With this method, the questions do not come across as interrogation, but rather as searching together. It is this second method of asking questions that is discussed in this chapter.

Viktor Frankl gave a clear image of these two ways of helping. Frankl founded logotherapy, an approach to psychotherapy in which the central aspect is discovering meaning in life. Frankl wrote:

To put it figuratively, the role played by a logotherapist is rather that of an eye specialist than a painter. A painter tries to convey to us a picture of the world as he sees it, an ophthalmologist tries to enable us to see the world as it really is. The logotherapist's role consists of widening and broadening the visual field of the patient so that the whole spectrum of meaning and values becomes conscious and visible to him.[1]

The following conversation with Tony utilized questions designed not to paint his world for him, but rather to help him see his world more clearly.

T1: I want to talk about Number 12 [on the List of Topics for Conversations]—"A relationship that means a lot to me is...." Since my family's moved away I've found out kinda what I'm made of as far as the family's concerned, and I feel a lot closer to the whole family now that they are gone. And it will be interesting to see what happens when they move back—to see if things will get back to my sister bugging me again and my mom on my case all the time.

PW1: You have gained a real appreciation for all that your family means to you, whereas before you weren't quite aware of all that.

PW1: My effort here was simply to "name the tune" (as Marvin Knittel describes in chapter five, so Tony would feel understood and would continue.

T2: Yeah, I was a big boy at the airport, but when they got on the airplane and started down the runway I was a six-year-old lost in the shopping center again.

PW2: That was a feeling of being—it's not quite abandoned—but being separated from those you love—a lost feeling.

PW2: I used one of his terms—"lost"—and a couple of my own— "abandoned" and "separated"—to resonate with what I felt in response to his powerful image of the little child in the shopping center.

T3: Uh-huh, and I just learned to appreciate the relationship that I had with my family. My mother and I are very, very close, and my dad and I are not so close. And my sister—it was kinda touch and go before they moved, and now I just can't wait to see her.

PW3: I can really catch an excitement about getting together. A sense of love and closeness with your mother ...and a wistfulness with your father—that although there's a respect there and a caring, somehow you'd like that relationship to be closer.

PW3: There were a number of emotions Tony mentioned in T3. I chose to place the focus on the distance between him and his father, and Tony's implicit desire to do something about that.

T4: Yeah, that's right, but I don't know how to go about that. There are things in the past that I hold against him that I do my best to overlook, and then there's his personality itself. He's in a very high tension job, and he's very hard to get through to, and to really get him to sit down and listen to you.

PW4: There are a couple of things going, it seems to me. One thing is that you have some old grudges that you can't let go of, and a second thing is that you haven't found a way to talk so that he'll listen to you.

PW4: If there are two concerns mentioned, as in T4, and I don't know which is the primary one, I will often reflect both.

T5: The grudges. . .I think I can deal with. It's something that I'll never forget, but it's something that I can put aside so that I could get closer.

PW5: Is there unfinished business in terms of those grudges when you're setting them aside? Is that anything you need to talk to him about?

PW5: I am always un-comfortable when some-one talks about setting grudges aside rather than dealing with them. So I asked him a question designed to help him explore this area.

T6: Well, it seems like something that's pretty much out in the open between us, and we both know how the other one feels about it, and it's something that I know we try to avoid.

PW6: So when you try to avoid talk-ing about what is on both your minds, it's probably pretty hard to talk about anything else that matters?

T7: Yes.

PW7: But you both have a silent commitment not to bring it up.

T8: Yeah, I guess it's one of those things you'd just as soon let die.

PW8: But it's like killing weeds—it keeps springing up again. *[Pause]*

PW8: I pursued the grudge issue to the point

Okay, what kind of steps can you take, Tony, to talk so your father will listen to you, so you can get through?

where I finally understood we weren't getting anywhere, so then I went back to pick up the second concern in T4, namely, that his father was "very hard to get through to." I framed the question in terms of actions that Tony might initiate.

T9: Well, I don't know. When he's here—he makes it back to town once or twice a month for meetings and we usually have dinner—he'll talk to me and it's like he's looking right through me—like he's not really there. His mind is somewhere else, and I can understand it because of the tension of his job, but I know it's there and I just wonder what to do to cut through that.

PW9: What would happen if you put your arm on his shoulder and said, "Dad, I feel like you're not really here"? What would be the worst thing that could happen?

PW9: My questions were designed to help Tony explore the consequences of being up-front—of saying what he was feeling to his father.

T10: He'd probably just sit and look at me.

PW10: Sometimes you have to get a person's attention. How is it with physical contact with him—touch? Is that anything that happens between you?

T11: Oh, a hug when he leaves, sometimes.

PW11: That's an important step.

T12: Yeah, but there's things...I just want to help him when he's around—help him with his relationship with the family and with me and with himself, because he puts himself through a lot.

T12: Tony's love and concern for his father comes through strongly in this response.

PW12: Okay, I'm understanding better. Your goal isn't just to build a closer relationship, but to really assist him in a closer relationship with the entire family.

T13: Uh-huh, because he carts his work with him. You know, he brings it with him, and it's not always real nice.

PW13: You'd like for him to be freed from thinking about tasks all the time and begin to look at the importance of relationships, too.... You want him somehow to be able to enter that whole area of relationships.

PW13: Usually somewhere in my responses, I try to bring in the concept of tasks and relationships. Many people major in tasks and minor in relationships without ever having conceptualized what they are doing. Then later, when they look back on their lives, they realize they have made a mistake. Tony, of course, was already thinking about the priority of relationships. I simply wanted to give him some words that might help him think more clearly.

T14: He's—well, he drinks a lot and smokes a lot, but with the potential that he has he could be the president of his corporation someday, but the way he's going about it, he's killing himself.

PW14: And that's where the center of your pain is?

T15: I think so—seeing that he could do it, but not the way that's he's going about it.

T15: I found out that Tony was thinking about his father's potential not being realized.

PW15: In fact, when you say, "He's killing himself," do you see him really shortening his life?

PW15: A radical statement, such as "He's killing himself," needs a question to discover the meaning assigned to the statement.

T16: Uh-huh, and he does, too, but he doesn't seem to want to change it. He's talked a little bit about getting out of the business, but he's talked like that before. And with his background, I don't think it will be possible for him to withdraw himself and be happy, because the challenge is what he goes on.

PW16: I sense your really deep respect for your dad, Tony, and also that you are doing a great deal of hurting for him because of the things he's missing out on, and you feel helpless.

PW16: I wanted Tony to come face-to-face with his helplessness to do anything to make a difference with his father. When we feel helpless, we often express our anger, which Tony did in T17—anger which had been on the back burner for ten years.

T17: Uh-huh. We never did much when I was growing up—he was always so involved at this job, and it seems like now, maybe within the last year or two years, he's made an effort to make up for the things that we never shared. But it's about ten years too late, and he doesn't realize—or maybe he does, but doesn't want to—that I've got to go my own way now and the past is already gone.

PW17: And it's your feeling now that he's trying to lessen that distance between you that was caused by his being so involved in tasks as you grew up?

T18: I think so.

PW18: So part of the barrier is in you—you're saying, "Dad, it's too late." And I sense a lot of anger in this, and a feeling of being cheated.

PW18: The only way that Tony could get over his helpless feelings was to realize that it was himself he needed to change. This is the one area he has control over. My question in PW17, my statements here, and the question in PW20 were to help Tony look within. Although I don't quote Bible verses to Tony here, the biblical concept of reconciliation underlies my responses.

T19: Yeah, I guess there is.

PW19: Just like for ten years or longer you were reaching out to your dad, but he wasn't even close. Now, he's reaching out to you, and you're not so sure you want to. [*Pause*] Had you understood before, that the barrier was partly or maybe even mostly inside you?

T20: No.

PW20: How do you feel thinking about that right now?

PT21: I think it will open me up a little more—help me be a little more accepting of his position.

PW21: It seems to me there's a growing awareness with you right now, Tony, of your own pain all those years you were reaching out and your dad didn't reach back. And also now a growing awareness of his pain, that he knows that, and he comes here, and he reaches out, and somehow he's not able to touch you. And then maybe a deeper awareness on your part of your anger—that there's a lot you missed out on. But there's nothing in life that says it's too late, unless you say it's too late.

PW21: In this response I wanted to lay the groundwork—Tony's growth in awareness—as a basis for a decision that I wanted Tony to see as resting squarely on his own shoulders.

T22: Like as far as this goes, I see the relationship is gaining, but the tasks are still there.

T22: Tony picked up on the task-and-relationships concept.

PW22: Well, I've understood, at least partially, the concern, worry, fear, you have for your dad. I think there's fear there—that you're afraid he'll die early. He will, when he gets done with life, have gained a lot, but might have missed what's best.

T23: Well, we've had a few talks.

When I was home one weekend, we took off down the road with the dog, and he told me a lot of things then. I just told him you better start to enjoy everything you've got now while you've still got it. . . .

PW23: Did you feel listened to?

T24: Yeah.

PW24: I think you've got a good insight into the way your father communicates. He is very active, and that kind of person talks about things that matter when he's doing something. So when you go for a walk you have a better chance of getting through than when you are just sitting.

PW24: I tried to teach Tony something about learning styles here, namely that the tactile-kinesthetic learner talks when he's doing something, rather than just sitting. Tony was caught up in more important concerns. (A learning-style checklist and explanation are in Appendix B.)

T25: But it'll be—I think it'll be easier when they move back here, because I'll be closer to them, and hopefully my presence will make a difference.

PW25: You've taken some important steps, Tony. One example is when you said to your dad that he needed to start enjoying some of the things he has. That shows a caring for him. How do you usually go about expressing caring?

PW25: In many helping conversations I ask this question in one form or another; "What is your way of expressing caring?"

T26: Oh, I try to talk to him about things that he likes, you know. I ask him about his job and just make an effort to talk.

PW26: How about the communication of love between you? It sounds like it's there on both your parts—that you really do love each other.

T27: Yeah. It's there sometimes and it's not there sometimes.

PW27: Okay. Is there anything else you want to talk about before we stop? Anything we've missed?

T28: I don't think so.

PW28: Can you think of any way you will do things differently now? Do you view anything differently now that we've talked?

PW28: Sometimes near the end of a helping conversation, I ask a question like this to enable the other person to see if any new perceptions or commitments have emerged. Tony's response in T29 showed that he had been very open in our conversation and now saw the need for change within himself.

T29: I think the thing about the block in me, no doubt. The missing of the years, you know. I'm kinda shutting myself off now, and I think that really hit home a lot.

Tony has a lot of work to do, but he has the desire, and he has a direction. Questions can be useful in helping someone find a sense of direction. The following Guidelines for Effective Questioning may clarify some of the underlying reasons for my questions in the conversation above, as well as provide a rationale for questioning in other helping conversations. Each person is unique and will benefit from unique questions. However, there are some principles that can be generally useful, when applied in a flexible way.

GUIDELINES FOR EFFECTIVE QUESTIONING

1. *Not all responses should be questions.* One can ask too many questions when trying to help. Helplessness can result when the helper takes control of the conversation by asking a long series of questions. Question-asking skills should be only one of a repertoire of helping responses. Depressed persons, especially, often have difficulty responding to questions. Since they have very little energy, questions tend to wear them out.

2. *Questions should benefit the other's quest.* Our own curiosity is insufficient cause to ask a question when we are involved in a helping conversation. Since the other person is always working toward some kind of healing or growth, our questions need to honor and facilitate that quest. This, of course, means that we must listen with great concentration to hear even the whisper of a direction.

3. *Effective questions expand the other person's thinking.* Many people going through emotional trauma want to make a decision when they are least able to do so. They want to narrow their choices to one. The problem with doing this is that some good choices may not even be considered. A wiser way to make decisions is actually to expand one's thinking by bringing in many more possible options. Then, when we narrow our choices, we are more likely to make the best decision.

Questions beginning with "how" and "what" help people think in this way. For example, "What are some other possible alternatives, even though they may not look attractive to you at this moment?" or "How could you talk to your father in a way that would not cause him to be defensive?" or "What are some ways in which you could keep your job and not continue to be belittled by your boss?" Our peripheral vision tends to narrow when we feel threatened, so we need questions like these to widen our horizons. Gerald Corey has discussed this type of question:

One kind of question that I find useful is an open-ended, rhetorical question designed to generate some thought. I might ask: "What do you expect that you'll be like in five years if you continue as you are now?" "What is the worst thing that can happen to you if you take a risk and fail?" "How would you like to be different from the way you are now?" "What or who is preventing you from being a different person?" Questions that lead clients to search within themselves for honest answers are different from those that probe for information.[2]

4. *The best questions release rather than direct.* Every person has great God-given potential. The most effective thing we can do as a helper is to be part of releasing that potential. The List of Topics for Conversations, which served as the stimulus for many of the actual conversations in this book, is designed to release people. Some questions that may have a releasing effect are "Why not?" and "What do you need to do to become fully you—to start moving towards becoming all that God has in mind for you?" and "What would it take to begin looking up instead of down?" Fear, of course, is what bottles us up, encases us in a shell, and keeps us immobilized. Our questions need to challenge and attack that fear.

STUDY THE QUESTIONS OF JESUS
The conversations of Jesus provide us with many guidelines for our own helping conversations. I've found it useful to study these conversations, looking at them in many different ways. One of these ways is to examine the questions Jesus asked. Here are some of his questions:

- At the conclusion of the parable of the Good Samaritan, Jesus asked, "In your opinion, which one of these three acted like a neighbor toward the man attacked by the robbers?" (Luke 10:36). This is a releasing, motivating, thought-expanding question.
- When a man spoke up in a crowd to ask Jesus to tell his brother to divide his inheritance with him, Jesus replied, "Man, who gave me the right to judge or to divide the property between you two?" (Luke 12:14). This thought-

provoking question causes me to look at my own propensity for taking responsibility for others.

- After Jesus asked his disciples who others thought he was, he asked the questions, "What about you?...Who do you say I am?" (Mark 8:29). In his helping conversations, Jesus often used the "discovery" method, rather than the "telling" method. Even at this point—the central issue of his teaching ministry—he chose to release rather than control or direct his disciples.

Jesus asked many other questions. Whether you are going through this book on your own or with a group, you can have a pleasant diversion at this point by studying these questions. Just go through the Gospels and look for a question mark when Jesus is talking. Then ask yourself these questions:

What was the purpose of his question?

Did it accomplish his purpose?

How can you apply this kind of question in your own helping conversations?

LIFE-LAB

After this study, use what you have learned from it and from this chapter in framing questions in your conversations. Start slowly. The tendency is to overuse a skill when we are seeking to acquire or develop it. You will find that with a few skillful questions you can deepen the flow of most of your conversations.

People who do not value themselves often think too much, though not too highly, of themselves. They spend all day thinking about how terrible they are! Such persons who "look down on themselves" cannot even receive a compliment, let alone help themselves. Helping such a person is like trying to push a wet noodle—it gives the facilitator a feeling of impotence. How do we go about the difficult task of helping someone move from a negative to a positive view of self? The following two methods are presented in this section:

Affirming Unique Strengths
Helping with Tasks and
*   Relationships*

PART 3

REBUILDING A SENSE OF WORTH

EIGHT

AFFIRMING UNIQUE STRENGTHS

One way to help a friend move from a negative to a positive view of self is to discover and affirm his/her strengths. Discovery usually requires careful observation and listening. Affirmation is the communication of this discovery to our friend. The conversation below contains several affirmations.

I have known Brad for about a year. (This is the same Brad who talks in chapter two.) One of his distinctive characteristics is his quest for spiritual growth. As we scanned the List of Topics for Conversations, and talked about them, it became clear that Number 2, "A personal quality or strength I cherish about myself is...," was a relatively new area of thought for him. Therefore, I suggested we talk about it, and that idea met with his approval.

This is an unusual approach for me—to suggest a topic. But I knew about his desire for personal growth, and this triggered my suggestion.

PW1: In terms of a personal quality or strength you cherish about yourself, is there any characteristic that hits you right at the moment?

PW1: "Hits" may not be the best choice of verbs here. I think I used it because I intuitively recognized that Brad was a touch-movement *learner.*

Another, probably better, response would have been, "Are you in touch with special strengths you have?" Responses like these, which honor the other person's sensory modality, are often useful. (A learning-style checklist is in Appendix B.)

B1: *[Long pause]* I don't know if this is a good quality or strength, but maybe being independent.

PW2: Okay.

B2: I guess that's something that I've always prided myself on—that I haven't been one that has to always lean on somebody else.

PW3: Yes, it sounds like that's a trait that means a lot to you—something that's been with you for a long time.

B3: I think I grew up with that trait.

PW:4 Sounds like also you have a strong belief that that's the way to be.

PW4: My purpose here was to help him connect his strength with his belief system. This apparently was useful in helping him think and/or talk about a tension in his belief system. One's belief system usually determines one's actions. Therefore, it's often helpful to refer to beliefs.

B4: Well, I don't know for sure if that's the way to be completely—I think you need to be independent to some extent, but I think it's also important to be able to depend on other people and trust them.

PW5: Perhaps to be interdependent.

B5: I imagine I've had a harder time doing that. It's easy for me to be independent. It's hard for me to be interdependent, as you say.... With my personal life there were times when I would not in the least way try to reveal too much of myself to somebody. One of my best friends sat next to me in high school almost a year before we even started becoming friends....

PW6: So, self-disclosure on your part has come hard?

B6: Yeah, but in doing it, it's also brought about a lot of freedom.

PW7: The freedom sounds like something you cherish about yourself. What other qualities do you think of, Brad, that you really value in yourself?

B7: I think maybe it would be my moral beliefs. I really value and cherish them. My belief in God, and belief in what he did for me—his love for me—those things I really cherish.

PW8: Your moral standards, the spiritual dimensions of your life, your relationship with Christ....

B8: And just seeing that grow. I really cherish that. *[Pause]*

PW9: Have you sat down to try to take an inventory of your strengths before?

PW9: I sensed some discomfort with Brad (later identified by Brad in B10 as "awkwardness"). Therefore, I chose to change the direction of the conversation from a pursuit of the topic to the appropriateness or legitimacy of the topic.

B9: No.

PW10: How does it feel doing that?

B10: Awkward—just thinking about it. I guess I never thought about it before.

PW11: Now, "awkward," what would some of those feelings be? Like it isn't quite right to do it?

B11: Yes, you know, like maybe you'd be bragging—not really sure if that's a quality someone else sees or just something I *think* I have.

PW12: One area that it seems to me you have special strength in is honesty—straightforwardness. Is that something you see?

B12: Something I strive for. I really do. I guess when I was twelve or thirteen—I can't remember if it was a pastor or just—somebody said that God hates liars and they quoted a verse—so I really have worked at trying to be as honest as I can, and it's still kinda funny 'cause sometimes, you know, I'm not. I had to swallow my pride here a few weeks ago and ask someone to forgive me of that, so even though I strive to be honest there's still times where I guess I'm not.

PW13: Do you think it's all right to go ahead and talk about strengths that you have, or does that violate your conscience? Do you think it's showing too much pride to do that?

PW13: I was still concerned with whether Brad thought it was appropriate to discuss his strengths, and I felt the need to get explicit permission from Brad to continue this discussion. In our helping venture, we need to be sure that we are not invading privacy or violating conscience.

B13: No, I think it's good that you know what your strengths are and what your weaknesses are.

PW14: One of the things I see in you is that you really have a quest to grow.

PW14: This response was based on B6—growth in self-disclosure—and B13—growth in honesty.

B14: It really is...something I want. One thing I would like to do is continue to be a growing Christian until the day I die—and to help others grow.

PW15: That's another important strength that you have—a commitment to helping others. That's a very strong mission with you.

PW15: If I had not listened to the very end of B14, I would have missed the sense of mission evident in the last few words.

It's important not to start planning your response while your friend is talking. Wait until the last word of his or her response to begin forming yours. Question—what if I don't know what to say? Answer—Admit it.

B15: Yes. Somebody has helped me and made it easier for me to realize who I am in Christ and to grow, and I guess I want to pass it on.

PW16: That relationship to Christ you alluded to several times—that's a very vital part of your life—that connection. *[Pause]* Now as you just let things surface in your mind, Brad, what other kinds of strengths or special abilities are you seeing?

PW16: I used a visual image here: ". . . as you just let things surface . . . what . . . are you seeing?" Also, my gesture in PW17 provided a visual representation. Even though your friend's learning preference may be touch-movement *(as I think Brad's is) or* auditory, *the use of a* visual *image, stated or actual, is worth trying.*

B16: *[Pause]* I don't know.

PW17: Well, it may be that even though you have given yourself mental permission up here *[I pointed to my head]*, down in your heart there's still a block somehow—to letting yourself see them. What we've been talking about is making a strength inventory. It sounds like you are a growing person, but that's probably one avenue you haven't explored very much.

B17: I guess maybe that illustration is right. Even though my mind has told

me it's all right, my heart still hasn't
received that, because some of the
strengths I was thinking of weren't
strengths that I see myself as having,
but that other people told me that I
had.

PW18: That ties in, I think, with
what you were saying earlier, that
you tend to be very self-reliant or
independent, which meant that sometimes you did not trust others. So if
others told you, "Brad, these are the
strengths I see in you," you might
have not believed them, or you were
somewhat doubting of what they said
to you.

*PW18: I thought we were
getting very close here to
the center of Brad's difficulty in identifying and
accepting his strengths.
His life-style of trusting
himself but not others
was a barrier to accept-
ing their affirmations. I
wanted to draw that
connection. Whenever we
can, it's helpful to tie a
"weakness" to a
"strength." They are
usually quite close to-
gether.*

B19: Yes, that's true, because people
have told me—my wife and others—
that it's real easy for me to relate to
the people in the Sunday school class
I teach—but I have a hard time seeing myself as a teacher and, after-
wards, here I am wondering if it's
any good at all.

PW20: Now, when they tell you that,
do you believe them?

B20: I don't know. I've grown to
accept it.

PW21: You don't *disbelieve* them.

B21: Yes, I don't disbelieve them; I
just don't know if I can accept it,

because I don't know it for myself. I don't know it as being fact.

PW22: Well, it looks like part of the struggle you are involved in is it's hard for you to believe good things about you.

PW22, 23: My aim in 22 was to pinpoint where I saw Brad as being right now, and in 23 to suggest a direction for growth.

B22: I think that's probably right.

PW23: Seems like that's a real growing edge for you—that you want to be more open to accepting your own strengths?

B23: I think it would probably really be helpful. I was reading somewhere that we have grown up with a lot of negative things. *[Pause]*

PW24: It could be that there is an adventure ahead of you in your life of discovering the gifts that God has given you—the strengths that you have—and to cherish them. It sounds like, from the feedback, you have teaching gifts.

B24: I don't know. *[Laugh]*

PW25: Are there any other strengths that you want to bring up now?

B25: I guess not—I don't really think so.

PW26: Okay. Can we talk a little bit about what we've been talking about? You've had some feelings—how have you felt since we've been talking about this?

B26: Encouraged.

PW27: Okay.... And awkward—have you had those feelings?

B27: Yes. Probably more so earlier than what I'm feeling now.

PW28: A feeling I sensed was that you wanted genuinely to see your strengths, but they weren't showing up like you wanted them to. My guess is that as you free yourself more psychologically to examine them, they'll probably just pop up to the surface of your awareness.

B28: *[Pause]* How would a person go about psychologically freeing themselves up more to accept those strengths?

B28: Yea! I consider this question the most important response of the session. When your friend asks you a "how" question relating to behavior change, he or she is showing insight, and at least a beginning commitment to change.

PW29: Hmmmm—well, let's brainstorm a little. *[Pause]* One thing I think of, Brad, is a belief that to be humble is not to compare—therefore, I should not compare myself to others—and to think that I'm worse or better than others is a comparison. So that when I find my strengths, I try not to compare them to anybody else's, and that's a relief.

Also, I believe that anything I have is a gift from God, and to deny that

PW29: I chose the word brainstorm because, first, I was caught by surprise by the question and needed time to surface ideas. Also, I like the word because it avoids a prescriptive or recipe approach. It is usually helpful, when asked, to provide suggestions rather than "take the following three steps...."

Also, I challenged

is like pushing a gift back at the giver.

Another thing for me is believing that others can see me better than I can see myself—that fish do discover water last. Therefore, I want to really try to trust people who are close to me. Virginia Satir says you go to a convention and you get a name tag. You look in a mirror and the name tag is backwards, and she says, "How do you know that everything isn't backwards?" It probably is—we just think we know how we come across, the strengths, the weaknesses, but probably those who are close to us do see us more accurately, particularly if there's some agreement in others' views.

B29: What if they disagree?

PW30: If two of my friends give opposite opinions, then I want to cast the deciding vote. *[We laugh]* But if two or three people tell me the same thing, that would be something else. ... Those are some of the thoughts I have about opening one's self to his strengths.

Also, Sid Simon says everybody ought to make up an "anti-suicide list"—fifty reasons not to kill themselves. We can do this in a positive way by writing down fifty things that we really cherish about ourselves.... I think maybe a part of it, Brad, is that you might need to begin affirm-

Brad's belief system on several counts. We need to challenge belief systems to bring about change, but that challenge needs to be given in a friendly way.

ing yourself before you feel comfortable. Just doing that will probably provide some release.

B30: It's been hard for me to discover other persons' strengths and to convey these strengths to them. I wonder if that isn't somewhat tied together?

B30: Brad's insight here shows that his "peripheral vision" is expanding. He is finding himself released to get more of the big picture and to draw connections. An expanding peripheral vision is a good indicator that growth or healing has taken place.

PW31: I think that's an important insight. As you free yourself to look at and affirm your own strengths, maybe you'll be better able to do that with others' strengths. And I think it works the other way, too. It's just a general skill—whether we do it with others or ourselves—the skill of discovering and affirming strengths.

Our conversation ended at this point. But as Brad was going out the door a little later, he turned around and said, "I think I'll begin a list of qualities I cherish about myself."

About a year after I had the conversations with Brad, which are recorded above and in chapter two, I received a letter from him that included the following progress report:

I have come to realize that I do have something to share with other people and I can help them. I still sometimes battle with rejection and the thoughts that what I have to say aren't important, but I realize that they are lies. I am beginning a systematic Christian discipling ministry helping people grow in their spiritual lives.

DISCOVERING AND AFFIRMING STRENGTHS

I have found that many people are like Brad was—they have not learned to celebrate the gifts God has given them. In fact, they believe it is morally wrong to acknowledge their strengths. It is useful to challenge and chip away at this belief system, because such a view holds people hostage to a lie, namely, that it is wrong to discover and affirm the good that God has placed in our lives.

Some years ago I began to puzzle about why only a few people were doing most of the work in our church. It was not that the others were lazy. They were competent, hard workers outside the church. I decided that most of the non-workers in the church did not think they had anything to give. Conversing with some of these members confirmed that point of view. I got responses such as, "I can see where some others have a lot to contribute, but I don't" and "What do you mean, I have teaching gifts? I don't see that at all."

So I decided to lead a Gifts Conference in the church, and later did this in a dozen other churches. We would spend a weekend studying Romans 12 and 1 Corinthians 12, to discover our gifts—and then make a commitment to use them.

This is one way to help people discover their strengths—assist them in doing a Bible study in this area. Another way is to do what I tried to do with Brad—learn to "sleuth out" these gifts through observing and conversing. A third way is to gently challenge others who believe that it is wrong to talk about their personal and spiritual strengths.

LIFE-LAB

This can be a very satisfying week, as you discover and affirm the strengths of several of your family members, friends, or fellow workers. It will be a week of gift giving. And you will find many people waiting to receive this gift of affirmation. A high-school teacher told about her experience:

I had a conversation with another teacher who seemed particularly washed-out on this occasion. We were talking about the seniors and what a trial the end of the year is for them. Without realizing it and certainly without forethought, I just happened into this situation. Looking back, I realize that I shifted gears mentally, from exchanging information to listening. It was obvious to me that the other teacher did not really mean the seniors—he meant himself. So I focused on his feelings, switched to "what" questions and settled back to listen. I asked what the end of the year looked like to him—what he thought he would have to be doing by then. He responded with a torrential listing of duties and responsibilities. He said he was afraid that he would not be able to get them all done, but I think what he meant was that he resented the amount of his own personal time that all these "things" would occupy. So I got out my calendar and we planned a few weeks, noting the empty spaces more so than the filled ones. As we worked, I commented on how easily his schedule fit together and how well-organized and sequential he always is, and, ultimately, how unselfish he is with his time. I reminded him that he had spent his Christmas vacation taking kids skiing in Colorado (including my twelve-year-old) and that he spends his weekends with the speech team judging meets (and he isn't even the sponsor) and teaching bridge to residents in our retirement home, and that most of his life he gives to others gladly.

This teacher went on to say she had discovered several rules in giving affirmations:

1. You must be totally honest in finding unique strengths and not just making nice remarks for the sake of making nice remarks.

2. This requires serious thinking because hypocritical comments come to mind easily, but an honest statement about another's strength requires noticing the other's strengths in the first place.

3. You must have concrete examples of what you mean, to offer as evidence, or you will not be believed.

I learned from this teacher how important it is to be concrete in affirming others. She gave her colleague a number of specific examples of his unselfishness and caring. Perhaps this conversation and the one with Brad, above, can serve as useful models for your ventures in "affirming," this week.

NINE

HELPING WITH TASKS AND RELATIONSHIPS

A number of psychiatrists, beginning with Freud, have said that we are mentally healthy if we are able to work and love well. Work and love have to do with the tasks and relationships of our lives. We know from experience that our feeling of self-worth is closely tied to a realization that we have achieved competence in our tasks and closeness in our significant relationships.

One of the fastest, most effective ways of helping people like themselves better is to help them become more competent in tasks or deepen their relationships. I do not mean by this that it is easy. When someone tells us, or shows us by his or her life without telling us, that he is suffering from a lack of self-worth, we may be able to help this person change his perspective by thinking with him about the quality of his tasks and relationships. Then we can focus our attention on helping such people improve the area with which they are most dissatisfied.

HELPING TO IMPROVE TASK COMPETENCY
I will use the example of a learning-disabled (LD) person to illustrate the improvement of task competency, because LD is

a widespread condition. Many children and adolescents (the statistics suggest between 5 and 15 percent) have some kind of learning disability. They may have inefficient visual or auditory sequencing ability, and therefore misspell words by reversing letters. Or, because of dyslexia or some other form of reading disability, they are not able to read well, even if they are quite intelligent. I have noticed by working with many learning-disabled children, adolescents, and adults that they need counseling as well as academic help. Otherwise, they tend to approach adulthood with a lack of self-confidence and sometimes with a lack of a sense of self-worth. The reason for this is that they have been going through life, especially their academic life, on "tilt." They cannot trust themselves to perceive accurately, and this lack of self-trust broadens to other areas of their lives. Thus, they often become excessively dependent on others, sending out "radar beeps" to check with other people on their own actions.

One such person was a college student. Liz came to see me because she was getting C's and D's in her classes, and the rest of her life was going about the same way. However, she ranked in the upper fourth of her age group on an individual intelligence test. Still, because she was "wired" differently, she was not automatic in addition or subtraction. When I asked her, "What is eight plus five?" I heard her tap her finger five times on the chair as she made her way mentally up to thirteen. Yet, she was a licensed practical nurse and was able to change medication figures from fractions to decimals and from English to metric equivalents.

Liz also had to think about which was her left and her right hand. She read very poorly and had literally faked her way through school. Because she could read a word here and there, and because she was bright, she could guess at the meaning of sentences and paragraphs.

It was not difficult to get other students to read her textbooks for her, nor to get some of her books taped for her by a "tapes for the blind" service. Her fellow students said that after one oral reading of Greek tragedies, she knew who murdered whom, and after one reading aloud of basketball rules, she could pass a proficiency test in that area. In other words, her auditory-oral channel was quite efficient. So she went from C's and D's to A's and B's. But another predicament persisted.

Although Liz could not read books well, she had learned to read people quite accurately. For example, she would get a teacher to stand beside her because the teacher would give clues to a right answer in ways the teacher herself did not understand. Liz had learned to depend on others to know what was "right." She even had to have someone sit in the passenger side of her car when she parked diagonally, to make sure she was parked at the correct angle and at an appropriate distance from the car on her right. Therefore, it was quite natural that she wanted others to guide her on most of the decisions of her life. She was unsure of herself morally because she had never been able to trust herself in the other areas of life.

As Liz began to improve in her schoolwork and especially as she began to find that she could trust her ears, she gradually began to gain faith in herself. She had known all her life what she could not do, but she had not known what she *could* do; that is, she had not been aware of her strengths— namely, that she was bright and was an auditory learner. It was important for Liz to talk about all those years when she had learned not to trust herself. She was one of those persons who "should not have made it" in life, but did because of her determination.

An important point to note about Liz is that it was only after she actually began to do better in her classwork that she began to regain some of the self-confidence and self-worth that she had as a little child, prior to starting school. To help people feel better about themselves, we need to find a way to help them achieve whatever it is they want to achieve. Then the good feelings come.

People will show us how to help them if we observe them and listen to them closely. Most learning-disabled persons are now identified and referred at an earlier age for testing and treatment. However, they still need help from family and friends to work through predicaments similar to those Liz encountered. It should be noted here that everyone with a learning disability has a unique set of problems and potentials, not necessarily like those of Liz.

GUIDELINES FOR HELPING PEOPLE BECOME COMPETENT IN TASKS
There are several helping ways that may prove useful when working with friends, regardless of their specific blocks to competency:

1. When they show that they lack self-esteem, talk with them about what they are doing that is not at a level of competency with which they are satisfied. It may be typing, assembly-line work, playing the piano, schoolwork, using a computer, carpentry, dieting—in short, any task that is significant to them.

2. See if they are willing to make a commitment to become competent. If they are not "sick and tired of being sick and tired," they will probably not change. Sometimes I say at this point, "It will require a great deal of hard work and courage for you to become competent in doing this. I don't know if you are ready to make such a commitment. Are you?" If they are unsure about the commitment, it is useful to say something like, "It's probably best not to work toward this goal of competence until you are hungry for change. Otherwise, you will become frustrated too easily and quit."

3. If your friend decides to change, then work very hard to discover and point out his/her areas of strength.

4. Find out what kind of help, if any, your friend needs in the pursuit of excellence. You may be useful in finding written resources or people resources or both. What your friend is doing is initiating and carrying out an "adult learning project." Malcolm Knowles, one of the outstanding adult educators in America, has spent most of his professional life helping people implement their own individual learning proj-

ects. His method works, whether one wants to become an amateur astronomer, a word-processor operator, or a skilled helper.

One of Dr. Knowles's books is a small paperback classic entitled *Self-directed Learning*. He points out in this book that the main purpose of education can no longer be to transmit what is known.

In a world in which the half-life of many facts (and skills) may be ten years or less, half of what a person has acquired at the age of twenty may be obsolete by the time that person is thirty. Thus, the main purpose of education must now be to develop the skills of inquiry.[1]

The Knowles method of self-directed learning is a straight-forward one. First, we decide what it is we need to learn. Next, we specify some precise learning objectives. Then comes a very important third step—mapping out a strategy for learning and deciding what people and/or written resources to utilize. Finally, we need to produce the evidence that we have indeed learned what it is we wanted to learn, and we may wish to have one or two friends verify our learning from their point of view.

I used Knowles's steps last year when I decided to use a word processor in my writing. The first step was clear enough—what I needed to learn was how to use a word processor. My three objectives to begin with were to buy the "right" one for me, to learn how to use the software to do two things—write a manuscript and write letters—and, fi-nally, I wanted not just to copy material from a yellow tablet or typewritten page to a word processor, but actually com-pose on it. My strategy was to buy the word processor and learn how to use it when one of my adult children, Bill, was home on vacation. He would be my primary resource, but since he lives out-of-state, I wanted to gain some familiarity with the user's manuals so I would have a resource when he was gone. With Bill's help, I did the above steps and was producing manuscript material and letters the first day. I thought the quality was satisfactory, and he verified that.

I have had to revise a part of my plan. The manuals are, from my point of view, less than clear. So I've had to get help a number of times from my wife, Lillian. (Bill taught her how to use it the same time he taught me and noted she remembered the instructions better.) Or, if she does not know how to do a certain thing, I go to the people at the friendly computer store. I have gained considerable proficiency in using the word processor, and I am now fairly efficient in composing on it.

Adults spend hundreds of hours a year on individual learning projects. If we follow a method such as Knowles's, we will gain confidence in our ability to tackle effectively many new areas of inquiry and to help others do the same.

HELPING TO IMPROVE RELATIONSHIPS

We have been discussing how we can help a friend improve his/her self-concept by increasing competency in a significant task. What about people who are feeling badly about themselves because they cannot seem to build close relationships? This is also a difficult predicament with which to help someone.

I have noticed that this is often the case with those who suffer eating disorders, such as anorexia nervosa or bulimia, referred to by Marvin Knittel in chapter five. These disorders are at a near-epidemic level in some colleges, high schools, and junior high schools. Anorexia is characterized by a weight loss of 25 percent or more, a ''drivenness'' to reduce calorie intake, and often an excessive urge to burn up calories through exercise. Most anorexics are girls or young women. They often stop menstruating, and their biochemistry becomes imbalanced because of lack of potassium and other essentials. Bulimics go through a gorge-and-purge sequence, but their weight is often near normal. Both anorexics and bulimics often have a high standard of excellence for tasks. They may be doing schoolwork, extracurricular activities, and other tasks very well from another's point of view, although their work usually does not meet their own demands for perfection. But their real predicament is in the area of relationships.

Cindy was a twenty-year-old who had been bulimic for about three years. She was doing many of the same things that other bulimics do—eating pounds of food at a time, then going to the bathroom and inducing vomiting. She would take a plastic bag to bed with her to vomit secretly at night. She took laxatives many times a day.

We began to talk about her relationships. They lacked intimacy. She was not satisfied with her lack of closeness with other family members, nor was she satisfied with her relationship with her boyfriend. Cindy was able to pinpoint two things that were causing her a great deal of pain. The first had to do with her lying and deceit to cover her gorging and purging. Since she was a person with a great deal of integrity, she was losing her self-respect by regularly practicing deception. The second source of pain was that she saw herself as "a good little girl" who did not "talk back" or even express her feelings when she had differences with a family member or friend, including her boyfriend. I have found that these two sources of pain are common, although not always present, among bulimics.

She began to discover as we talked that stuffing herself with food was symbolic of the way she had been "stuffing" her feelings for years. She was playing the tune that Marv mentioned in chapter five, "I'll Swallow My Feelings." She also believed that if she were to be assertive, it would not be tolerated by those close to her. It would be as if she was defecating or vomiting on them. Who could take that? Cindy decided to take the risk, beginning with her boyfriend. She "told him off," saying some things to him that she had wanted to say for a long time. She told me later that when she came home that night, it was the first time in months that she walked right past the refrigerator and went to bed. Before she went back that fall to her out-of-state college, she talked with each of her family members about differences she had with them. She had begun to move towards personal health by starting the process of straightening out her relationships.

GUIDELINES FOR HELPING PEOPLE IMPROVE RELATIONSHIPS

Here are some guidelines that can be applied generally with persons who suffer a lack of self-esteem because their relationships are distant rather than close:

1. Take the point of view that as people work to put integrity into their relationships, they will feel better about themselves. Insist upon integrity in your own relationship with a friend.

2. Listen desperately to what your friend is saying about his or her relationships. Listen to what he does *not* say. If he is lonely, he may actually be afraid of being with people. If this is true, he will find all kinds of reasons not to reach out to others.

3. See if he wants to target one significant relationship for a greater closeness. Remind him that it will take a great amount of energy to achieve this, and that success will be dependent on the other person as well as himself.

4. Provide honest feedback about your friend's strengths and needed areas for change.

5. Help your friend focus on his relationship with God. This relationship lends a spiritual quality to all other relationships.

6. Suggest to your friend that he spend time with children and learn from them how to deepen relationships. My book *Learning from Children* has a chapter on this topic and a chapter on an allied topic—friendliness.

7. Teach your friend to use tasks to deepen relationships. There are many tasks that can lend themselves to the achievement of this goal—for example, learning how to use a computer, doing the dishes together, and teaming up with someone to make a gift for a mutual friend.

LIFE-LAB

During your lifetime you have probably made many lists of tasks to complete. Have you also made lists of relationships you wanted to deepen? Think for a moment about family members, friends, fellow church members, people at work, and others. Which faces rush into your mind? Choose two or three people who often dance through your thoughts and target them for a closer relationship. It will call for a considerable time commitment, of course, to move them into an inner concentric circle toward the "bull's-eye" of a close relationship. But if we become as intentional about deepening relationships as we are about getting tasks done, we may be surprised by the results.

After you have thus begun with yourself, listen in your conversations this week for yearnings that people have to feel better about themselves—to rebuild their sense of worth. By using the guidelines given in this chapter, along with your own ideas, you may help them to become more competent in their chosen tasks and to develop a more satisfying closeness in some of their relationships. In these ways, you can help release them from a preoccupation with a lack of self-worth, so they can move on to concentrate on the spiritual dimension of their lives.

We can be most useful in others' lives if we get to the center—the core—of where they are living. When we focus on the spiritual dimension of life, we are at that center. Such a focus requires the helper to be dependent on the Holy Spirit for wisdom, love, and power. We begin to help others when we come to the end of ourselves and our own skills. Of course, there are times when we need to refer to a mental-health professional; but here I am talking about crises that are beyond *human* help.

We are promised the presence of God for just such risky situations. How may we utilize the vast spiritual resources that are available to us in the helping venture? Here are some paths which other counselors have traveled:

Using Our Weaknesses to Help Others
Using the Bible in Counseling
Utilizing Other Care-Givers
Using Metaphors and Telling Stories

PART 4

TUNING IN TO THE SPIRITUAL DIMENSION

TEN

USING OUR WEAKNESSES TO HELP OTHERS

We live in a world where it is important to be strong. We may even "fake it" to cover up our weaknesses. As a teenager we may act "cool" rather than admit we are scared. In middle age we may become a "stuffed shirt" to hide the contours of our real selves. However, our weaknesses may become our friends if we accept them as a part of ourselves. And they may prove to be a way to reach out to others. Compassion springs from the roots of our weakness. A middle-aged woman discussed one of these roots:

I vividly remember a most humiliating experience of my childhood. Mother sent me to the first grade when I was four and my sister was five. We were inseparable, and rather than make us both unhappy, my mother started us in the small country school together. I wet my panties in school because I was afraid to ask how to go to the toilet. The teacher spanked me in front of the entire class, then removed my wet undies and sat me on a little red chair over the furnace. I'll never forget the shame and embarrassment I felt, and the bad feelings concerning the teacher.

Most of us have a number of weakening experiences in our lives that we will never forget. These can be utilized in our reaching out to others. This woman is now a very effective

counselor. She is at her best when she works with those who
have been diminished as human beings by emotional trauma
or physical illness. Her "woundedness" has made possible a
healing touch to alcoholics, the very ill, dying, bereaved,
lonely, and many others.

We have a clear model for utilizing our weakness in the
service of others: "You know the grace of our Lord Jesus
Christ; rich as he was, he made himself poor for your sake,
in order to make you rich by means of his poverty" (2 Corinthians 8:9).

The apostle Paul builds on this paradox in the same
epistle:

*Three times I prayed to the Lord about this [Paul's physical
ailment] and asked him to take it away. But his answer was:
"My grace is all you need, for my power is greatest when you
are weak." I am most happy, then, to be proud of my weaknesses, in order to feel the protection of Christ's power over
me. I am content with weaknesses, insults, hardships, persecu-
tions, and difficulties for Christ's sake. For when I am weak,
then I am strong. (2 Corinthians 12:8-10)*

Little children seem to be "content with weaknesses." They
live in a world of giants (adults), so they can identify with
other little beings and show them special compassion. Children are especially attracted to baby animals and small pets
and often show special kindnesses to them. These little animals thus benefit from a child's "weakness."

Walter Wink has written about the viewpoint that our
weakness can become an avenue on which we move toward
helping others. In his useful book, *Transforming Bible Study,*
Wink asks questions about the biblical story of the Good Samaritan. One of the questions is:

*Who are the "wounded" in our society today? Who are the
"robbers"? Without getting sidetracked on the question of
whether we should stop on the highway for disabled cars or*

hitchhikers, what would we bring to actual wounded people or groups of people if we were in touch with the Samaritan aspect in us?[1]

The "Samaritan aspect in us" is our own weakness or woundedness. The Samaritan knew what it felt like to be cast aside, shunned by others, and afraid. He therefore reached out with the caring he would have welcomed for himself. He loved a "neighbor" as himself.

Rollo May, an internationally known psychoanalyst and author, has discussed the "wounded healer": "Out of the chaos of neurosis, psychosis, or physical illness there can come as a response to the challenge a new level of greater understanding, greater compassion for others and greater empathy...."[2]

Henri J. M. Nouwen capsules the "working from weakness" concept in his powerful little book, *The Wounded Healer:*

For the minister is called to recognize the sufferings of his time in his own heart and make that recognition the starting point of his service. Whether he tries to enter into a dislocated world, relate to a convulsive generation, or speak to a dying man, his services will not be perceived as authentic unless it comes from a heart wounded by the suffering about which he speaks.[3]

WHY BE AWARE OF OUR WEAKNESSES?

As noted above, we can identify with others and accept them, if we are aware of our own weaknesses. In addition, we can reach *out,* rather than *down,* to help others. We can be accepting, not judgmental. This is true when we are able to accept our weaknesses as part of the human condition. Paul Tournier has spoken eloquently to this point:

One of my patients was a woman who had undergone a long and unsuccessful course of treatment by a psychoanalyst, followed by the equally unsuccessful intervention of a Christian

*healer.... But the trouble was that she felt so ignorant beside
the learned psychologist, and so unbelieving beside the believer.
...If I do not succeed in convincing her that I am essentially
as weak as she is, everything I have to say to her...will be
only one more crushing lecture for her.*[4]

Another advantage of weakness is that it renders us de-
fenseless and thereby open to others. The weak of the
world—little children, the very elderly, the poor, and the
sick—are vulnerable. When we admit our weaknesses, we
become vulnerable, and the relational life-style becomes possible. We know we need to receive as well as give. And it is
only as we admit our weaknesses that we can begin to receive help from others.

DISCOVERING OUR OWN WEAKNESSES
A beginning place for each of us who wants to be able to
respond to others' needs is to identify some of our significant
weaknesses. Probably most of us can list these faster than we
can list our strengths. Some of my own weaknesses are:

1. I am a worrier.

2. I did not like or accept myself when I was about thirteen years old. It was not until I was in my thirties that this
part of me was healed.

3. It is important for me—*too* important at times—to
please others.

4. I periodically have a "crisis in my confidence," during
which time I am convinced that I am teaching my classes at
the college very poorly, and I would be doing my students a
favor by leaving. However, the evidences are that I do a rea-
sonably good job of teaching, even during the periods when I
lack confidence. The problem is that at these times I tend to
evaluate my competence in a negative and inaccurate way.

Knowing I have these weaknesses (and these are not the
only ones; they are just the first ones that came to my mind)
helps me better understand why and how I can reach out to

others. A common theme I see in my weaknesses is that I need to trust God and to trust the process of living one day at a time. I am working to do this. For example, I have worked successfully to reduce the frequency of my "crisis in confidence." My Renewal Support-Training group (described in chapter eighteen) has given a big boost to my confidence level. Also, when I feel my confidence shaken, I usually go to Marv Knittel or another good friend and say, "Help!" I find that I need a periodic counseling outlet.

If I succeed in correcting these and additional weaknesses of which I am aware, I will surely discover other weak areas that need strengthening. Perhaps, as we climb a bit higher in our moral-spiritual development, we are able to see more of the "territory" that needs work.

LIFE-LAB
Here's a change of pace for your Life-Lab work this week. Instead of focusing on others, spend some time studying yourself. Reflect on your own weaknesses. List a few. In your conversations with friends, ask them to tell you about your weaknesses. Be sure to tell them the purpose for this request. Add these to the list you have started. Then apply these questions to this list:

1. Do you see a common theme?

2. Can you accept yourself—weaknesses and all? Or do you brood on your imperfections?

3. Are there steps you can take to begin to correct these weaknesses?

4. How can your "woundedness" release you to assist others in theirs?

As you discover your own answers to these questions, and attend to the resulting ricochets in your mind, your counseling effectiveness will increase.

ELEVEN

USING THE BIBLE
IN COUNSELING

It is important to utilize the Bible as a resource in counseling. On the other hand, it is not helpful to "beat people over the head" with verses of Scripture. How can the Bible be used so as to show respect both for it and for the person with whom we are working? The conversation below provides an example of this approach.

Ted, a thirty-year-old man, came wanting to talk about Number 26, "My spiritual growth. . . ." In his own words, he was a former "Jesus freak" who "fell completely away from religion and stopped attending church for a long time." Now he is married, has a two-year-old daughter, is active in church again, and wanted to take a new look at his spiritual life.

T1: I don't want to be superficial in my Christian life, but it's all ill-defined for me at this point. . . . I'm hoping this conversation will help me define some things.

T1 and PW1: As noted in other conversations, the first statement of the counselee is very significant. When possible I select a word from that statement that gets at the primary concern. Then I use that word to "join" the other person in my response. This time I resonated with "define" which Ted used twice.

PW1: Well, it seems like part of the definition for you is that spiritual growth means that you do not want to compartmentalize your life....

T2: Yeah, I feel if I'm going to believe, I should believe it twenty-four hours a day and in all locations....

PW2: You mentioned definitions, Ted. How do you define a Christian? What does that mean to you?

T3: Well, I think to really be a Christian, you have to believe in Jesus Christ as your personal Lord and Savior, you know, belief in God, the Holy Spirit, the Apostle's Creed, all that.... But it has to be "soul deep," it's gotta go all the way down.... That's what a Christian needs—is to have that deep commitment.

PW3: So commitment is central. Now in Mark 12, a lawyer asked, "What is the greatest commandment?" And Jesus replied, "The greatest commandment is that you should love the Lord your God with all your heart and strength and soul and mind, and your neighbor as yourself." This means to me that the center of our commitment is to relationships—relationships with God

PW3: When I use a biblical passage in a counseling session, I try to select one that "fits" with the counselee's goal. Instead of using many biblical references, I usually use one, then come at it from different directions.

and with our neighbors. I would guess our families are our closest neighbors. How do you feel about your spiritual relationships, like your relationship with God?

T4: Well, okay, uh, I'm not, not lately, a person that reads the Bible a lot, and I feel I need to increase that sort of thing. I have a lot of time commitments right now with my church activities, graduate classes, and work. I put off spending time studying the Bible and that sort of thing, so there's room for improvement, but I think I've made some improvement, too.

PW4: Is that something you want to change? To spend more time with God?

PW4: This response was a check on motivation level.

T5: I think it would be good for me to do that because I feel that a Christian should have that type of a commitment....

T5: Ted's response is characterized by duty rather than desire. I think a sense of duty is very important in a relationship, but it isn't enough to make the relationship flourish.

PW5: Do you view your relationship with God as a duty rather than as an attraction?

T6: Yeah, I guess I never would have thought of it that way. I feel like the Lord has given me some talents and abilities, and that I should use those. ... I don't think that to believe in the Lord you have to be in the church, in the building itself, in a Bible study or whatever.... I need to spend time preparing for a career, and I want to spend time with my music.... It's a serious hobby, it sometimes makes me money, and it's my release.

PW6: That's an interesting word, because that seems to me to have so much to do with the Christian life, and with spiritual growth—being released.

PW6: I was pleased to see Ted go beyond duty to being released in at least one important area of his life—music. And I chose to explore the idea of release with him. The importance I attach to being released is based on biblical teaching generally, and specifically on John 8:36: "If the Son sets you free, then you will be really free."

T7: Yeah, I think that release is really essential to what I'm looking for as a Christian. I want to feel that release, like, "I'm a Christian. I'm doing the Lord's will and, boy, it feels good!"

PW7: Can you identify what would need to happen in order for you to be *more* released?

PW7: I asked this question to help Ted begin to deal with his resistance to change in this area—to help him discover what his obstacles to change were.

T8: Well, right now I'm busy, and I think, Where's the money for the bills going to come from? Am I going to get a job when I graduate? I feel like I'm so tied up with all these other things that I haven't got time to read the Bible and...maybe I can just kinda hold on to where I'm at until a better time.

PW8: So there's a time-and-money bind and a lot of pressures. So probably your life is more centered now on tasks than relationships. Have you learned anything yet from your two-year-old about life or about spiritual life?

PW8: The biblical background for this question about his two-year-old daughter is Matthew 18:3: "I assure you that unless you change and become like children, you will never enter the Kingdom of heaven." Having a general knowledge of biblical teaching can be very useful in giving direction to one's helping responses, even if we do not quote the verse aloud.

T9: Well, one thing I've found is when I take the time with her—doing the things a two-year-old does—playing, making some faces, and funny noises at each other, and playing in the sand with her—that I have a lot of fun. I find myself just laughing and feeling like a kid again myself.

PW9: Your face brightens when you start talking about spending time with her.

T10: Oh, yes, it's a release, you know, and I find myself getting kind of disappointed in myself that I don't take time to do that more often because it is a neat feeling to sorta let out my child, and I *want* to do that

T10: There was a wistfulness present in this reply—a real desire to live life.

more. The same with my wife. I've been really irritable lately just because of all the things that are on me, and something has got to change, because I don't need to put that on her. She has enough problems with the things that she does.

PW10: I can catch the fact that you do feel guilty because you've been less helpful, and more of a problem to your wife than you would like to be. When you say you want to spend more time with your daughter and be more kind to your wife and read the Bible more, you sound like the carpenter who didn't take time to sharpen his saw because he was so busy.

PW10: In chapter thirteen, "Using Metaphors and Telling Stories," I discuss the value of metaphors, such as the one here about the carpenter and the saw.

T11: Yeah, that's exactly right.... I know it, and it's not quite clear to me how to get that all worked out, but I know there's got to be a way, and I've got to find it.... I guess I feel like what I really have to do is to first worry about finding a job, I mean one that would support us better, if it's at all possible to find one. I may have to put off graduating for a year or two. It wouldn't kill me, but the bills may do us in; the money thing is a very critical thing now.... The payments get behind ... and my wife, it affects her....

T11: Ted communicates his desperation in this response. His desire to change and his trapped feeling are made clear here.

PW11: I think I'm understanding a little better where the pain is in your

PW11: Once we can help the counselee localize the

life. There hasn't been enough
money, and part of the pain is that
this has gotten between you and your
wife—when you really need each
other more than ever.

*pain—find out where the
hurting is—the counselee's
thought processes usually
begin to clear. His very
first response was ". . . it's
all ill-defined for me at
this point." Pain befogs
our thinking.*

T12: Yeah, and we find ourselves
arguing about money.... Some of
the arguments are so petty. Later I
think, "Why did I complain about
her doing that?"...

PW12: It seems like you have a pretty
clear idea about what to do about the
tasks in your life—look for a job that
will bring in more money. Do you
have a plan for the relationships in
your life?

T13: Well, I need to continue to
spend time with my daughter....
The best thing is not to get myself
tied to the TV; I tend to say, "Oh,
I've got to see this movie on TV."
Well, I can live without the movie,
but I can't live without my daughter
and my wife.... But I think marriage has to grow over a period of
time....

PW13: Part of the feeling that I get is
that there is some distance between
you and your wife. Is there any part
of you that says you need to make
that right, straighten it out?

T14: That's a very good thing because we have been arguing quite a bit lately....

PW14: I would think it would be hard to work on your spiritual growth if there are things you need to work out with your wife.

PW14: The biblical background for my response here is 1 John 4:12: "No one has ever seen God, but if we love one another, God lives in union with us, and his love is made perfect in us." This passage seems clear to me—if we want to grow spiritually, that is, grow in our union with God, one way to go about it is to love those near us.

T15: Hmmm. Yeah, I hadn't really thought of that, but that probably is a big part of it.... I don't feel that it's severe. My wife has a lot of respect for me and I have a lot of respect for her....

PW15: Maybe you haven't been saying that to each other a lot?

T16: I don't think we've said it enough....

PW16: Probably in the time it would take for a commercial or two on TV you could say things to your wife that you need to say. *[Pause]* We've talked about a lot of things. As we wind down...which of those things seem most important to you?

PW16: Why did I give him this free advice? Probably because I had neglected to say some affirming things to my wife that day.

T17: Well, the family thing...I guess I get so caught up with things that I just don't put down the burden long enough to take care of the family business and things that I should....

PW17: What could release you to do what you need to do with your life? What is keeping you from it, besides time?

T18: Well...part of it is that I just don't take time for myself and my thoughts....

PW18: So that you get out of touch with yourself and your life?

T19: I'm so caught up with *doing* that I'm not taking enough time to *be*.

PW19: ...It seems to me that your relationship with your daughter is going very well, but you are wondering about your relationship with God and yourself. Your daughter can teach you a lot of things about slowing down and just being you, and about instant forgiveness...and it seems to me a frontier for you right now is the need to work on lessening the distance between you and your wife. Then you will be able to move on to a closer relationship with God.

PW19: When I'm working with a person who lives with a master teacher (a little child), I want to be sure he (the adult) is teachable.

T20: ...It strikes me now that I'm looking ahead for the peace and contentment that I hope to have in my life later on, and maybe I'm overlooking some things that I could do right now....

T20: I thought this was a very important discovery that Ted was making here. He speaks eloquently for all of us who need to stop brooding about the future and begin to make

PW20: Okay, is there any commitment that you're ready to make now in terms of changes? I'm not talking about huge things, I'm talking about starting small and beginning promptly.

T21: Well, I think the first obvious thing is to take a little time to think about things and what needs to be done, and then maybe to sit down and to share some of those things with my wife, because it's when I don't share the planning with her that we have conflicts.... Today some of these things got a lot straighter in my mind because I talked to you about them, and it's one of those things where talking to you helped me spend some time with myself.

the most out of the present moment.

PW20: Ted, early in the session, talked about the importance of commitment. Therefore, it seemed fitting to invite him to consider making some commitment at this point.

The way that I used the Bible with Ted is representative of the way I generally use it. You may want to develop your own style of referring to Scripture, if you have not already done this. Just as each of us has a unique style in all that we do, so a part of that style will be the way we refer to the Bible in our counseling and helping. Your style will be determined by your general life-style and helping technique, and by your beliefs about the Bible. My own belief is that the Bible is the Word of God, so I deeply respect the wisdom and power that come through its use.

GUIDELINES FOR BUILDING A BIBLICAL BASE FOR COUNSELING
There are several guidelines that I have found useful in developing a biblical background for helping others:

1. *Make a commitment to spend a lifetime in inductive Bible study.* It is crucial to find out what the Bible says. For me that means I need to approach it in an inductive way. In this context, *induction* refers to the process of reasoning from a part to a whole, from particulars to general. This process, of course, differs from *deduction* in which we take a premise and then reason to its conclusion. In the inductive approach, we start with the actual words of the Bible and work from these "parts" to the "whole"—what that passage is saying.

My way of beginning to find out what the Bible says was to take time out to go to seminary. There I was helped in the quest by many excellent teachers who taught me how to study the Bible inductively. Now, I am not suggesting that everyone take time out for in-school Bible study, although I benefited greatly as a layman. I am recommending continuing study on your own and with a group to discover biblical truths and ways to apply them. When it comes right down to it, you either take someone else's word for what the Bible says, or you discover it for yourself.

Two booklets on inductive Bible study are *The Joy of Discovery in Bible Study,* by Oletta Wald,[1] and *Firsthand Joy,* by Rick Yohn.[2] Both these helpful references describe and apply the inductive approach. If you like to listen to cassette tapes, I recommend that you consider Bible Believers Cassettes, Inc. This loan library, started by Ed and Gaye Wheat in 1963, has thousands of taped Bible studies, recorded by pastors, theologians, and other Christian leaders. Tapes are sent on a donation basis to all fifty states and over twenty-five foreign countries. A catalog is available.[3]

2. *Work to "prescribe" a given reference for a given need.* To fit a biblical reference with a human, spiritual need requires thorough knowledge of the Bible and discovery of the person

with whom you are talking. It is important to me to have in mind some major *themes* of the Bible. One of these is the "relational theology" of the Bible. This is the reason I used the Mark 12 passage with Ted, in the conversation above. This passage is perhaps the most succinct reference concerning the centrality of relationships in the Christian faith. Therefore, I put this together with Ted's need for spiritual growth and used the passage as a backdrop for our conversation.

Another example of a biblical theme is *creation*. The Bible begins in the very first verse (Genesis 1:1) by recording the remarkable creative energy and acts of God. The first attribute of God is seen to be that of Creator. Since we are created in God's image, we can be sure that creating is meant to be a part of our lives. We see continuous creative bursts in childrens' lives that serve to remind us of this heritage.

Creating is a spiritual experience. The finished product and often the process itself bring us a sense of accomplishment and joy. At the completion of creation, "God looked at everything he had made, and he was very pleased..." (Genesis 1:13).

John Claypool describes it this way:

As the process of creation unfolded, God looked at his adventure of joy and was overwhelmingly pleased with what he had started. The Hebrew text almost pictures God as a little child rubbing his hands together in relish and jumping up and down as he says, "It is good! It is very, very good!"[4]

Sometimes we can help others by releasing them to create. If they have shut down their creativity, they are unlikely to be as happy as they could be. If I sense this, I usually refer to this biblical passage and ask when they last created something that made them feel like dancing. Then I ask what it would take for them to be released to create again. What someone creates, of course, has to come from his/her own imagination. It might be a painting, a poem, a special meal, a stained-glass window, or an exciting backyard. And that initial creation need not be a great, time-consuming one. It simply

needs to be the first in a renewed, creative way of living.
With Ted, I built on his reference to music, not only as a way
to be released, but also as a way to find joy through creating.

There are many other biblical themes, such as grace, love,
reconciliation, forgiveness, and courage. I suggest you make
your own list of major topics in Scripture. You will be much
more likely to refer to the themes if you have inductively
found them from your own Bible study. You can use these
ideas to touch something very deep in the persons with
whom you work.

3. *Biblical references need to be used naturally.* I have not felt
comfortable going into a helping conversation with an agenda
of Bible verses or references to use. It seems to work best for
me if they surface naturally in the flow of conversation. As
noted above, the needs of the person will help bring a reference to mind. But timing is also an important factor. If someone is telling his/her story, it does not seem right for me to
interrupt with a quotation from the Bible. If there is a great
deal of emotion being expressed, it may be better to wait. The
words of the Bible are so important that they should be used
at a time when they will be listened to.

4. *Biblical references should be used to express God's love.* The
senior pastor of a large evangelical church told me once that
he had learned a great deal from an eight-year-old girl, who
always had some comment or observation when he was shak-
ing hands with people after church. She looked up at him
one Sunday morning and said, "Pastor, there are more people
who come forward when you tell us about the love of Jesus
than when you scold us."

Love is, of course, the outstanding theme of the Bible.
Many people are hurting and need to know they are loved.
This is what provides healing for the past and present, and
hope for the future. We have the opportunity of being the
channel of God's love by pointing others to that love, and by
living it. I think Gary Collins put it well in his excellent, in-

depth resource book, *Christian Counseling: A Comprehensive Guide:* "Jesus, therefore, had two goals for individuals: abundant life on earth and eternal life in heaven." These two goals can provide direction for Christian counselors.

LIFE-LAB

Here are three steps to consider as you work this week to develop the skill for effectively using the Bible to help others:

- In your daily Bible readings, take note of those passages that are making a positive difference in your life. Commit them to memory, or write them on a 3-by-5 card to carry with you.
- Think of a few of the people you will be talking to this week. Think especially of their *needs.* Do these people especially need to mourn, laugh, celebrate, grow, or heal?
- Then, when you are with one of these family members, friends, or fellow workers, listen attentively to what is said. Also listen for Bible verses that the Holy Spirit may bring to your mind during the conversation. In this way, you will be able to match a scriptural resource with a human need. The Bible verse may remain unspoken, but you will be guided in your response by it. Or you may choose to share it with your friend as something that has made a difference in your life and may be useful in his or hers.

One of the verses I have found helpful in my life and that I sometimes pass on to others is 2 Timothy 1:7: "For the Spirit that God has given us does not make us timid; instead, his Spirit fills us with power, love, and self-control."

This has been a valuable resource many times for me when I have felt timid and afraid. And that is one of the values in utilizing the Bible as a resource—we are thereby brought into the presence of God and can then respond with newly felt courage.

TWELVE

UTILIZING OTHER CARE-GIVERS

I have found that many people are like me, in that we feel we need to carry out tasks by ourselves. Where did we get that idea? Did we learn in school that collaboration was cheating? Or have we learned in life that we must "carry our own weight"? Or is there still a myth of the frontier that we can depend only on ourselves? Whatever the cause, many of us do not seek the assistance of others when we try to help a friend. Sometimes there is a reason for this—confidentiality—but often this is not a factor, since many know when a person is in grief, is divorcing, or is suffering from anxiety.

MATCHING HELPERS WITH PEOPLE WHO NEED HELP
We cannot help every person who needs help. Not only do we not have time, but there is also another element. For some reason we may not "hit it off." This may have an irrational or unseen basis, such as transference. I may remind a man of his brother, whom he never liked, or of someone else with whom he is conflicted. There may be other reasons. This person might profit more from talking with a woman than with a man, or with someone younger or older than I am. Or a special mentor may be needed, with skills I do not have.

A fairly rigid woman (her own diagnosis) wanted to become more spontaneous and playful. Together we decided that children are master teachers in this area. She then spent several half-days a week for three or four months as a volunteer aide in a preschool. She worked hard at playing, and "got down on all fours" with the children. Although her knees became a bit callused, she became softer, more flexible, and more expressive.

In situations like these, the original helper may be regarded as a broker or networker. The skills that I put to use included the following:

1. I needed to be able to listen well enough to discover a goal she wanted to work toward.

2. I needed to know what strategies, resources, and experiences would help her reach her goal.

3. At this point I needed to be in touch with a network of resources so that I could connect her with a specific setting—in this case, a preschool.

4. It was important for me to have the skill of being supportive to her during the process. Usually, when people do something that is healing for them, it is also uncomfortable for them at first. Therefore, they may need encouragement to continue, or someone to talk with concerning the "strange" experiences and new feelings they are having. As it turned out, this particular woman had a very strong quest for growth, which was enough to keep her going until she got "hooked on" the fun she was having.

5. The skill of evaluation or verification is important for the helper at this point. Following her experience in the preschool, we evaluated her learning and growth, and I was able to verify and affirm the positive changes in her beliefs and approaches to life.

6. The final skill was that of planning ahead for continued learning and growth towards this person's goal as she worked at it on her own. This woman decided to keep her goal of becoming more spontaneous and playful as a high priority. She was going to keep in contact with little children, al-

though not in such a time-consuming, organized way. She was going to practice being herself with other adults, rather than spending a lot of time thinking about how she should be.

GAINING THE NECESSARY MATCHMAKING SKILLS

Except for the third one, the above six skills are covered in other parts of this book. They involve careful focusing on the other person, along with appropriate responding. Number 3, the matchmaking or brokering skill, requires the ability to *network*. John Naisbitt, in his book *Megatrends,* has referred to the increasing importance of networking in our informational society.

Networks exist to foster self-help, to exchange information, to change society, to improve productivity and work life, and to share resources. They are structured to transmit information in a way that is quicker, more high touch, and more energy-efficient than any other process we know.[1]

To do some of the things mentioned by Naisbitt, such as exchanging and transmitting information, fostering self-help, and sharing resources, we need to become knowledgeable about the resources that exist, particularly those in our own community, or we need to know how to find these resources rapidly. If we know the existing resources, we can usually connect a person with a helper in one phone call. If we are not familiar with all the resources—and probably no one is, even in smaller communities—we can usually do the matchmaking with two phone calls. The first call is to another person with a network knowledge. For example, if a retired friend says he wants to learn to be a portrait painter, your first call could be to an art teacher in a high school. If another person has been a "doormat" all his life, with one or two phone calls we could get him connected with a resource for assertiveness training. Still another person may be getting deeper in debt. By a phone call or two, we could set up financial counseling, sometimes free, with a credit union, bank, or other financial institution.

It is useful to think in terms of strategies and resources. Many communities have human-services resource directories. These are very useful to have on one's desk. Knowing the adult-education courses that are offered by the local school system or community college can also prove valuable. Most valuable of all are the friends you have. Consider the expertise they have in many different areas. For example, your pastor may be an expert concerning the many resources for spiritual growth in the community.

LIFE-LAB

One way to begin improving your networking ability is to think of some of your friends and acquaintances. What are their "hot buttons," or special interests? Do you have two friends with the same "hot button"—improving helping skills, writing poetry, reading detective stories? They might profit from knowing each other. Do you have one friend who is in difficulty because of unwise financial decisions, and another friend with training and background in money management? My experience has been that most people are altruistic and willing to help others if they know a need exists.

If you are not yet prepared or ready to begin networking, I suggest you use your Life-Lab time this week to seek out a *mentor* in this area—someone who is highly accomplished at matching people in need with others who have resources to meet those needs.

I have had two mentors with this skill for a number of years. Both these men have an almost uncanny knack of connecting people in such a way that each person benefits. These two men seem to be thinking "people resources" all the time. Each of them has connected me with several people who have had a significant impact on my life. In one case I was networked with a person halfway across the country.

Observe your friends carefully, and when you discover a superior networker, "tag along" and you may find yourself developing those same skills.

THIRTEEN

USING METAPHORS AND TELLING STORIES

Some people prefer a logical, straightforward response to their statements. Others like a word picture. Those who prefer the latter need a helper who is able to use metaphorical language. One dictionary gives the following example of a metaphor: "The ship *plows* the sea." A metaphor lets us instantly "see" something that would take a long string of words to describe if the metaphor were not used. In the following conversation, I respond often with metaphoric language because of several clues that my partner in conversation prefers the method.

Grace wanted to talk about Number 26, "My spiritual growth...." I asked her about her concern in that area.

G1: I don't know if it is a concern; it may be more of an exploration of where I'm at, where I'm going, where I want to be.

PW1: Do you have any map for the territory you want to explore?

PW1: One way to join or connect with people is to build on one of their key words. I did that here with "explore." The metaphoric terms "map" and "territory" were also signals that I was trying to see her world.

G2: Well, I think I'm still in a learning stage. I want to learn more about my own spirituality....

PW2: Hmmm. Okay. You mentioned the exploration—do you have a direction about the way you want to be going personally?

G3: I really feel that I want to do a lot of teaching, perhaps conducting seminars.

PW3: What are the steps that you need to take in terms of your own spiritual healing or growth in order to be useful to others in those ways?

PW3: The word steps *here fits in with* exploration *and* direction, *terms we had used previously.*

G4: I think the biggest problem I'm facing now is my weight problem. If you talk about a healing or some kind of a spiritual completion, it would be that. It's a real problem for me.

G4: Grace's word completion *is a significant one. It says she believes that there is not enough of her in a spiritual sense. This differs from her physical being, where she feels there is too much of her. I chose in the next response (PW4) to build on the word* completion.

PW4: And so, your completion—that's an interesting idea in terms of wholeness. That is, your weight is keeping you from being the kind of a whole person you'd like to be.

G5: Yes, I'd definitely agree with that ... definitely true.

PW5: Help me understand how that's a barrier from your point of view.

G6: Well, it's kinda like how can I say something to someone or how can I present something to someone if I haven't made it work for me?... If I'm dealing with alcoholics or anyone with an addiction or a compulsive problem...you know, how can I say to them, "This works," if I can't somehow get it to work for me?

G6: Grace explains here her struggle with the issue of credibility.

PW6: You use the word *compulsive*. Is that how you feel?

G7: Umm-huh, I really do, definitely. I think it's compulsion...a compulsion to eat, even a compensation for things not satisfied.

PW7: Let's explore that a bit. As you look at yourself and you see the compensation for things not satisfied, what do you hunger for besides food?

PW7: I continue to use the term explore *since that was a part of her purpose statement in her first response. My question, "What do you hunger for besides food?" is a metaphoric way of building on her striking phrase, "a compensation for things not satisfied."*

G8: I would say love. I mean I've really explored that a lot. Love, just a total, accepting love, an unconditional love....

G8: Our "exploration" has taken us to the center of the territory, a hunger to be loved unconditionally.

PW8: And so there's a yearning and hungering to be loved just like you are? And could it be that you have

PW8: I wanted Grace to see what connection she was making between this

come to believe that if you could be loved as you are, that you could then change?

hunger for love and her ability to change.

G9: Yes, I would say that's true... that I wouldn't have to prove anything to anybody. I wouldn't have to go to food for satisfaction....

G9: This paradox seems often to be the case—when people don't require us to change, we are thereby released and motivated to change.

PW9: You'd be fulfilled.

G10: Right; I'd be fulfilled.

PW10: What do you see as a barrier or barriers to your being loved or accepted like you want to be loved and accepted?

PW10: I asked this question to discover if she saw the obstacle to being loved as being placed in her path by herself or by others. I think she takes quite a bit of the responsibility by bringing up her inability to deal with anger (G11).

G11: I've thought about it a lot, and I know anger is there preventing me. I have a real hard time with other people's anger, and somehow anger means to me, "No love," because I experienced a lot of anger as I was growing up with my parents. And now, especially with my husband, his anger is just something I cannot deal with. Whenever there's anger, I feel unloved...and there's still a lot of anger towards me from my mother because I don't hold on to her.

PW11: She didn't want to let you go?

G12:...I think she wanted me to stay part of her, close to her with all my problems....

G12: I missed a significant statement here. Grace was reinforced by her mother for having problems. Grace would be dependent, and her mother would take care of her problems for her.

PW12: She saw you as an extension of herself?

G13: I think when I was growing up that's probably very true. I don't think I had my own personality or separate identity.... I never thought of that before but that's true.

G13: Grace makes a discovery about her early days ("I never thought of that before"), which I wish I would have stayed with, rather than going on to a related topic.

PW13: When did your own identity develop?

G14: I think after I was married. I was forced to have an identity of my own. *[Pause]*

PW14:...Let's see, it seems to me the issue is that when someone's angry with you, you feel unloved.

PW14: Sometimes a pause can be a time to try to center again.

G15: Yeah, that's just a feeling I get. And probably...I've thought about it a lot—why I feel that way. And I think it's because when I love...I love very deeply, and I think unconditionally...so when others don't give me that same value, I have a real difficult time with it. And anger

G15: The terms wither *and* die *are powerful metaphoric terms.*

is one way I just totally wither. It's true, I die inside.

PW15: So, do you feel a need to please people a lot? Is that part of this situation?

PW15: I like to focus on needs. It seems to be an effective way to help people change.

G16: I'm so much my own person, but I've begun to discover parts of me that really do want to please other people. For example, I've been going to school and I've got degrees on degrees. And I thought about "Why am I doing that?" And it just dawned on me that perhaps that's one way to please. . . . I must be doing it for some level of acceptance from others. You know, if I'm not getting their love at this level, maybe I'll strive to get it at another level. I don't know if that makes sense or not.

PW16: It makes a lot of sense. . . . I'll tell you a story. It may be one that you know about. It's the first fairy-tale story that I can remember. There are many different forms of the story.

    A father and son were riding to market on a donkey. The older man had a sack of wheat under his arm. They met someone who said, "That's too much weight for a donkey," and so the father had the son get off, and they continued their trip. They met another traveler who said, "Here you are—an adult riding and your son having to walk. That doesn't seem

PW16: I was able to relate this story since I was a fellow struggler, another people-pleaser. I'm sure I remembered this story because it was a life theme for me. . . . At the end of the story, I asked if there was anything she identified with. It is important when telling a story to let the other person draw his or her own connections.

very kind of you!" The father then got off the donkey, had his son get on, and they continued on.

An animal lover came by and said, "Why is it right for you to walk unburdened, and have an animal that's burdened?" So the father had his son get off, and they both walked beside the donkey. A second lover of animals came by and said, "This animal has been carrying burdens all his life. Don't you feel guilty?" At that point the father, who always had tried to please everyone, had his son help him lay the donkey down and tie his legs together. They put a pole between his legs, then hoisted the pole to their shoulders, and carried the donkey, now upside down, into town. A crowd gathered to watch them enter the marketplace and jeered and laughed at them. Several said, "Look at those two—they're carrying a donkey! Have you ever seen anything so foolish?" As the father adjusted the sack of wheat on one shoulder and the pole on the other, he said to his son, "I've learned that I cannot please everyone."

Now, Grace, is there anything in this story that you identify with?

G17: Well, I immediately picked up on the "weight and the burden" because I knew how the story ended. You know, I could reflect on that,

G17: I was surprised. I had thought she would immediately pick up on the people-pleasing. She

and the two words that just came popping out at me were the "weight" and the "burden," and I never thought about the pleasing other people as much as carrying a weight and a burden. I don't know what that means, but that is just what came out to me.

identified with something closer to her, a "weight and a burden."

PW17: That's an interesting thought. And you are saying that you are carrying a weight and a burden?

G18: Well *[laughs]*, I am carrying weight—I don't know about a burden....

PW18: I'm wondering why those words jumped out at you.

PW18: "Jumped"— another metaphor.

G19: I don't know...I really didn't think "weight and burden of what?" ... It could very well be the weight and burden of pleasing other people ... that's very possible.

PW19: It sounds like it is important to you to avoid anger.

PW19, 20: I was working pretty hard here to draw a connection—perhaps too hard.

G20: Oh, absolutely.

PW20: And that can keep you busy trying to keep everyone calm....

G21: And everybody happy, yes, oh absolutely; I'm a great "keeping everybody happy" person. *[Laughter]*

G21: One of Grace's many strengths is her nondefensiveness. Because of her integrity and her motivation for spiritual growth, she is willing to take a hard look at herself.

PW21: Well, there's a lot of good to be said for that, but it does seem like it has been somewhat of a burden for you.

G22: Yeah, I'm not allowed to be angry. My husband doesn't allow me to be angry. . . .

PW22: What do you mean, you're not allowed?

G23: He would tear me down.

PW23: You mean he would say something. . . .

G24: That would tear me down, yeah. . . .

At this point Grace discussed her husband's use of sarcasm and how she tried to avoid it. Later, in a second session, she told how she had been assertive with her mother that week without being unkind to her. She also talked about her need for perfection, and I tried to help her shift the meaning of perfection from "without flaw" to "wholeness." We talked about her self-appointed task of smoother-of-the-waters in her family. She said she was getting close to resigning from that job. Then she discussed her need for a support group to hold her accountable for weight control. Yet, she had difficulty trusting others. I believe we got at the center of her spiritual need when she spoke of her difficulty in trusting God.

We stopped our conversations after two sessions. She had achieved the goal she stated at the beginning—"an exploration of where I'm at, where I'm going, where I want to be."

These sessions were awareness-building conversations. I believe she will later move on to the next steps of healing, commitment to change, and change itself.

The above conversations contain logical responses as well as metaphors and a story. The metaphorical response style evoked laughter and tears, and perhaps discovery.

AN ANCIENT TRADITION OF HELPING

There is a very old tradition of helping through the use of metaphorical language. Bruno Bettelheim reports the value of stories in helping:

This is the reason why in traditional Hindu medicine a fairy tale giving form to his particular problem was offered to a psychically disoriented person, for his meditation. It was expected that through contemplating the story the disturbed person would be led to visualize both the nature of the impasse in living from which he suffered, and the possibility of its resolution.... The fairy tale is therapeutic because the patient finds his own solutions, through contemplating what the story seems to imply about him and his inner conflicts at this moment in his life.[1]

THE EXAMPLE OF JESUS

I decided to go to the Gospels to discover how Jesus used both the logical method and the metaphorical technique in his conversations and teaching. To find this, I analyzed the Gospel of Luke, using *The Bible in Today's English Version*. I studied just the verses in which Jesus was talking, that is, in which quotation marks are used. Each verse was classified as *L* for a logical statement or *M* for a metaphorical statement. There were examples of both in the temptation of Jesus. Jesus' first answer to the devil is in Luke 4:4: "The scripture says, 'Man cannot live on bread alone.' " This involves the use of a metaphor, so I classified this as *M*. In answer to the second temptation, Jesus' response (4:8) was: "The scripture says, 'Worship the Lord your God and serve only him!' " This was a logical, explicit statement, so I classified it as *L*. Most of Jesus' statements were readily classifiable as *L* or *M*. Often, parts of the same conversation would contain different modes. For example, 18:24: "How hard it is for rich people to enter the Kingdom of God!" is *L*. The next verse, "It is much harder for a rich person to enter the Kingdom of God than for a camel to go through the eye of a needle," is *M* since it is metaphorical. All of Jesus' parables, or stories, are classified as *M*. But Jesus sometimes asked an *L* question or made an *L* statement at the end of a story. For example, at the end of the story about the Good Samaritan: "And Jesus concluded, 'In your opinion, which one of these three acted like a neigh- bor toward the man attacked by the robbers?' The teacher of the Law answered, 'The one who was kind to him.' Jesus replied, 'You go, then, and do the same.' " (10:36, 37). These two verses were classified as *L,* while the parable itself was classified as *M*.

Findings. In the Gospel According to Luke (TEV), there are a total of 583 verses which contain Jesus' words. There were 277 verses (47.5 percent) classified as "logical" and 306 verses (52.5 percent) classified as "metaphorical."

Implications for teaching and helping. After I did this study of the Gospel of Luke, I came to understand in a new way the appeal and power of Jesus' helping and teaching. He used both logical and metaphorical approaches and, in fact, often integrated them in a single conversation or homily. In this way he achieved some powerful experiences for his listeners. Obviously, his power came from the fact that he was the Son of God. Yet, Jesus was also a human being, and it is useful to understand the methods he used to communicate. If he used a combination of logical and metaphorical approaches in this venture, it is well worth our following his example. It is thought-provoking that some brain researchers are saying that "peak experiences" occur only when the logical and metaphorical approaches are integrated.

SPECIFIC METAPHORIC INTERVENTIONS
Some of the following examples of metaphors occur elsewhere in the conversations in this book. Others do not.

1. With a woman who had gone from her growing-up home to her first marriage to a second relationship, with little or no time in between—"There is an old saying that if you crawl from one nest to another, you will never learn to fly." Incidentally, since men as well as women do this, I have also used this metaphor with men.

2. With someone who was feeling guilty because she did not see the nature of the predicament she was in—"Fish discover water last."

3. With someone whose level of motivation to change was unclear—"Are you sick and tired of being sick and tired?"

4. With a father who wanted to parent differently than his father and grandfather parented—"Can you break the chain?"

5. With one who had some latent resentments against his parents—"Do you have any unfinished business to take up with your parents before you go on to the new business?"

6. With those who are trapped by their shyness, fear, anger, or hatefulness—"There is a saying, 'The shell of an egg is so thin that you can live in it for a lifetime and never know you're on the inside.' If that is where you are, what is your shell made of?"

7. With someone who thinks he knows himself quite well when the evidences do not indicate that to me—"When we look in a mirror, our name tags are reversed. Is it possible that there is a lot more of us than just the name tag that is unclear as we look at ourselves?"

8. With someone who is seeking internal healing or spiritual growth—"I've asked lots of people to sculpt how they see

God looking at them. Suppose God had a body and was looking at you. Would you stand now and take the stance that
you see God using for this?"

There have been many different sculptures of God. By far
the most common one has been a person with a grim facial
expression, and extended arm, and a pointed, wagging
finger—the universal expression of accusation. This is a tragic
misperception of God. The New Testament is clear that it is
Satan who is the accuser, and I point this fact out to persons
who sculpt God in this way. Others have had God standing,
peering down, again rather grimly, with hands on hips. Others have seen God with arms extended and waiting to wel-
come and embrace, much like the father of the Prodigal Son
in Jesus' parable. Whatever form the sculpture takes, it allows
me to start where the other person is in terms of his/her
view of God. It is my belief that I will not be very effective in
helping others discover a biblical view of God unless I first
understand the view of God they now have.

There are many other metaphors that I use other than the
ones above. You have scores of others that you use every day
in your conversation.

LIFE-LAB
As you talk this week, notice the figures of speech you and
others use. Begin to use some of these intentionally. The aim,
of course, is to listen so intently to the other person that you
can choose from among the metaphors available to you the
one that expresses "in a nutshell" where the other person
is—or needs to be.

As you relive your conversations, consider making a list of
metaphors, stories, and other figurative language. They can
become important tools in your helping ventures.

Twenty-five years ago, when I was learning to counsel, the emphasis in training was on helping the counselee gain insight: "If people get new insights, they will begin to change." I discovered soon enough that while insight was useful, it did not necessarily bring about change. I had to admit to myself that there were entire areas of my life that I knew needed changing. However, I was not taking any action in some of these areas.

Today one of the emphases in most counselor education is helping people overcome resistance to change. We can nearly always count on the fact that those who want to change are also resisting it. Otherwise they would already be changing.

The following skills are discussed in this section:

Identifying and Removing
    Obstacles to Change
Challenging
Resolving and Mediating
    Conflicts

PART **5**

OVER-COMING RESISTANCE

FOURTEEN

IDENTIFYING AND REMOVING OBSTACLES TO CHANGE

The following conversation tells the story of Robyn, a twenty-year-old woman, who wanted to talk about Number 18 on the List of Topics for Conversations—*A person to whom I need to say "I love you" is.* . . . Most of us are brothers and sisters of Robyn. That is, we, too, have felt that deep universal tension that comes with the realization that when we want to express our love to those closest to us, there is some opposing force within which resists that expression. I sensed this in talking with Robyn and, at times, focused my responses on these barriers.

R1: A person I need to say "I love you" to is. . .my brothers. That's a concern I have, too. . .my family. Ah, just growing closer to them. . .there's so much feeling in each of us and we just close it up. I got a letter from my older brother, and so that's the second letter I've gotten from him, so that was kinda neat. *[Laughs]*

PW1: It does seem to be awfully hard to say "I love you" to somebody

PW1: *I wanted to bring up the notion of resist-*

close...and with your brothers, uh, like if you think here you are and there's where you want to be, having said to your brother or brothers, "I love you," what do you think is the resistance...what's that mountain or obstacle made of?

ance immediately, and I did so by this response, and by sketching the drawing while I was talking.

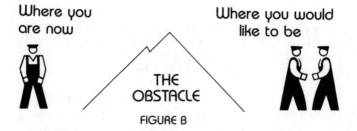

Where you are now

Where you would like to be

THE
OBSTACLE

FIGURE B

R2: I don't know. Sometimes I picture like...oh, they're gonna...they'll just ignore me the rest of my life, and I know that's not true!

R2: A very powerful "fear picture" or image.

PW2: A possible rejection.

R3: Yeah, a rejection. But like I say it to my mom over the phone just before I say good-bye—"I love you!" And she says, "Yeah, same here." Oh, man, that took some guts. I said that last night. I haven't said that for a while. I was so fired up, we had such a good talk, that I thought, okay, I'm gonna do it! Do some risking here. But then like when I wrote my brothers, I just put "Love ya."

R3: Enthusiasm—being "fired up"—helps one risk.

PW3: So writing might be a start.

R4: Yeah. 'Cause in the first letter I got from my brother, he just signed it, just his name, that's all. I thought, Wow! That's *personal,* you know. *[Laughs]*

PW4: *[Laughs]*

R5: And then this time he had "Love" right above it.

PW5: Where will you find your courage someday, when the time comes to just say to your brother, "I love you"?

R6: From just—just being fired up about something.

PW6: Because that helped last night when you were really excited.

R7: Um-hmm.

PW7: I think that what you want to do is very important. And I believe you'll find your way. Do you think you or your brother would be more embarrassed if you said, "I love you"?

PW7, PW10: My sequence of responses here was to help Robyn see her brothers' needs and strengths.

R8: Maybe that's why I don't say it. See, one of them's kind of shy. And the other one doesn't have much patience. *[Laughs]* Oh, I don't know, oh—

PW8: I think you're getting at something significant, because maybe you've been protecting your brothers.

R9: Yeah.

PW9: Do you see them as fragile—needing that kind of protection?

R10: I think they wouldn't know what to do because, well, I keep thinking that they know that that's missing in the family, since I've been away from home, and now since they have.

PW10: So their awareness probably is growing?

R11: Yeah, that's what I was thinking.

PW11: The need for communication.

R12: Yeah.

PW12: I think you've got a lot going there. And it sounds like maybe a part of that obstacle is your sensitivity to their feelings, and you've thought—

PW12: It was important to let Robyn know that one of her own strengths (sensitivity to others) was forming part of the barrier to her expression of love.

R13: Yes, I don't want to hurt them or make them feel uncomfortable. *[Laughs]* Yeah, that's probably it!

PW13: And it seems to me that you're at another place now, that there may be a cost to saying, "I love you," and that cost may be that one or both of you will feel uncomfortable. Are you willing to walk right into that, if you really believe that communicating your love is more important than your comfort zone?

PW13: This response took the form of a challenge. I considered it a gentle confrontation, one that would strengthen our relationship.

R14: Um-hmm. I do that sometimes. I just go ahead and do it, and then it's okay.

PW14: Like last night, when you said, "I love you."

R15: Yeah, and I have to say, "I'm gonna do it. Now don't blow it; let's do it"—kind of pump myself up. But we'd have to be in a really talky situation before, or I'd wind up probably crying or something—ahhh *[laughs]*.

R15: I love Robyn's enthusiasm and her choice of words! "Talky"?

PW15: Is that a part of your resistance to saying, "I love you," that you don't want to cry in your brothers' presence?

PW15: The fear of crying is often a big block to the expression of love. Crying is an involuntary response. We are "out of control" when we cry, and most of us fear being out of control. Also, we may have reason to believe it causes discomfort to others.

R16: Probably, that's probably part of it.

PW16: So, you're protecting yourself some, too. You don't want to show a weakness in front of your brothers, is that it?

R17: Oh *[laughs]*, I never thought of that.

PW17: There's some reason you don't want to cry.

R18: I know, there's some, humm *[pause]*, I think it's just because our

family has fallen into a pattern—
that's the way we are, and it would
be a change.

PW18: Okay, so you know what to
expect, and even though it's not as
close as you want, still everybody
goes with how things are, the status
quo.

R19: But I think we have gotten a lot
closer. We don't talk about feelings,
but we talk about things.

PW19: So, you're closer than you
used to be. How'd that happen?

R20: I think just us maturing, or
getting away from home, made it
happen, because we have more things
to talk about. And just being away
from home and coming back, you
realize how much the family means
to you.

PW20: There are a couple of things
that surface for me, Robyn. One is, I
think you want to protect your brothers from being embarrassed, and
another is, you're not sure what
crying in front of them would mean
for you, or perhaps for them.

*PW20: I wanted to leave
Robyn with a view of two
important blocks to
change.*

R21: Both.

PW21: Yes, both. They might not be
able to handle it or you might not be
able to. *[Pause]* Well, I believe in
what you want to do, and I think
you'll find your way. I don't think

*PW21: I can't show Rob-
yn the way—the pathway
to the expression of love
is different for everyone,
so each of us has to find
our own way. Yet, the*

you'll be comfortable, but it may be one of your richest experiences.

helper's role is important in bringing about needed change—when it comes to changing, "You alone can do it, but you can't do it alone."

R22: Um-hum.

I finished the conversation with an even deeper respect for Robyn than when we had begun. She had become aware of a deep need in herself and her family and was beginning some hesitant but courageous steps to overcome her resistance and to meet that need.

BLOCKS TO CHANGE

Sid Simon, who has led many workshops on values clarification in different parts of the world, says concerning resistance that there are usually a *number* of blocks to change. He has noted several of these:

1. Inertia ("It's not so bad").
2. An inability to exert our will.
3. We don't believe deep down we deserve any better.
4. We don't know how to seek creative alternatives.
5. We often don't know how to get the cooperation of others.
6. We aren't sure what we really value.[1]

As I look through this list for a common factor, the word *afraid* emerges. "I'm afraid to change." "I'm afraid I don't deserve any better." "I'm afraid to ask others for their cooperation in helping me change." "I'm afraid I can't control myself and my will."

Fear can keep us from connecting with another person, as discussed in chapter two. It can also keep us from making needed changes in our lives. As I write this, I realize I have been dealing today with my own resistance to writing. Deep down, I have been afraid to write, afraid that what I have to say will not be worthwhile. That fear has made me deeply resistant to change—to beginning to create—and it has been a part of every writing project I have undertaken. Fear also periodically accompanies my teaching at the college. Often, before going into the classroom, I think, "These students have invested a great deal of time and considerable money to take this class, and I'm afraid I don't have what it takes to make it worthwhile for them." Sometimes this feeling or thought is just for a moment, sometimes it lasts for a while. I have been helped by reading Rollo May's little book, *The Courage to Create*. May says that such anxiety accompanies all creative acts. Therefore, we need to overcome our resistance each time we create. Lately, I have been thinking that resistance and fear often melt before love.

LOVE DRIVES OUT FEAR

A group of college students with whom I work has helped me understand the relationship between fear and love. I have met with this Christian Supper Club of twenty-five to forty students nearly every Monday evening for thirteen years. Recently, we were studying 1 John, and I came at that time to understand 1 John 4:18 more clearly:

There is no fear in love; perfect love drives out all fear. So then, love has not been made perfect in anyone who is afraid, because fear has to do with punishment.

I am coming to understand that fear is not easily dislodged. It must be driven out! And, according to this biblical passage, the motivating force strong enough for this task is love.

This process—love chasing fear out of a life—is shown by Robyn's responses. Her choice of the topic itself: "A person to whom I need to say 'I love you' is..." was an indication of the power of love in her life. And in her first sentence (R1) she spoke of her desire to grow closer to her family. I worked to build on her motivation of love, for example, "Are you willing to walk right into that, if you really believe that communicating your love is more important than your comfort zone?" (PW13).

Another place where I could have built on her love would have been after R20. She said, "And just being away from home and coming back, you realize how much the family means to you." At that point, I chose to summarize. A more effective response would have been, "I sense in what you just said the very deep love you have for your family." This could have served to heighten the awareness and therefore the power of Robyn's love—and to give her more courage.

You have read through the conversation with Robyn and my marginal comments on ways I tried to help her overcome her resistance to change. Also, you have probably begun or renewed some thinking about the power of love to overcome blocks caused by fear. What are some other ways to help others conquer resistance?

Another way to overcome resistance is to help your friend create a plan for change. This plan can be a very simple one. Here's how it could work for you.

1. Pinpoint the exact change desired.
2. Identify the resources and strategies needed to make that change happen.
3. Work the plan.
4. Thank God for the change.

For example, you want to express your love to your parents, whether you are twenty and they are forty or fifty, or whether you are forty and they are sixty or seventy. First, *pinpoint* the change. Do you want to hug them, tell them, "I love you," or both? Or, when will you do this? You will need to create time, rather than wait for the "right" occasion.

Next, identify and decide what specific help you need. Would it be useful to have a friend along? Should you have your parents over for dinner? Do you need to write them first? Would it be helpful to make a list of some of the things they have done for you, so you *feel* the love more?

Then *work the plan*—carry it out. If you have not done this before, expect that it will take considerable courage. You will probably want to wait for a "better" time. You may cry, talk fast, or notice a quiver in your voice, but carry out your plan.

Finally, *thank God* that you have overcome resistance to change. The love and courage that made this possible are both gifts from God.

ACCOUNTABILITY

I checked back several months after having the above conversation with Robyn. The question I asked her was, "Have you followed through in getting better at expressing your love to your family?" She said she had done this with her older brother but was at about the same level as before with the rest of the family. She is excited at the deepening relationship she is experiencing with her older brother.

Checking back is a way of holding people accountable. It also gives the opportunity to reinforce an achievement and to give encouragement. I think my checking with Robyn will also cause her to resume work in this area with the rest of the family. Thus, holding people accountable helps reduce resistance.

A LOOK AT SELF

What are the areas in your life in which you are resistant to change? I had to deal with my own resistance to creating this chapter and admit that resistance before I could continue, with credibility. We bring not only techniques to the helping process, we bring *ourselves*. You will be welcomed as a fellow struggler by others if you are also chipping away at resistant areas in your own life. Have you found a way to release love and accountability in your life as an expulsive power against fear? Perhaps you need to talk with a friend about Number 23 on the talk-listen List of Topics for Conversations—*Something I need to change, but that I'm resisting changing, is....*

LIFE-LAB

The next step is to put the skills you are learning into practice with a friend who wants to change but is resisting it. This friend may be:

—wanting to go back to college, but resisting doing it.
—wanting to right a wrong relationship, but saying, "Oh, it's not so bad."
—wanting to express love to a family member or friend, but thinking, "That's something I can put off until the right moment [or year] comes along."
—wanting to make *any* change but resisting that change.

You will not have to *look* for people who are resisting change. Just be aware of what your friends are saying. Then listen, respond, care, challenge, love, confront, and hold accountable. Use all the skills we have been working on up to now. See if you can help your friend identify concretely the change he/she wants to make, and the block(s) to that change. Where does *love* fit in?

After the conversations, do the following:

FEEDBACK. Ask the persons you talk with whether the conversation was useful to them in beginning to deal with obstacles to change. Which of your responses were effective in helping them identify the obstacles?

JOURNALING. If you have found journaling a helpful way of living your conversation through a second time, let your memories of that conversation flow through your pen. Write the story of what happened and note the important transactions between you. Then underline, asterisk, or otherwise note some highlights. Which of your responses helped your friend deal with resistance? Did he/she change in any way because of the conversation? Did you?

REPORTING TO YOUR GROUP. If you have a small group with which to relive your conversation, report it in the same way you would have journaled. Compare your perceptions of the most effective transactions with theirs. You may wish to role-play some different ways of responding. Finally, ask the group to help you identify what you did that worked and what specific skills you need to continue to enhance.

PERSONAL REFLECTION. If you don't journal or report to a small group, relive the conversation in your thinking by using some of the questions I have asked under "Journaling" and "Reporting to your group," above. Work at being open to the ricochets in your mind as you read these questions.

CREDIT YOURSELF FOR EFFECTIVE RESPONSES. Crediting yourself for responses that worked helps cement those responses into your repertoire. It also enhances your confidence.

TARGET ANY CHANGES YOU NEED TO MAKE. I suggest you make a three-column chart, like the one below. Start with an easy thing to change in your own life. It's fun crossing off an item on a list! Then, having met with initial success, you can go on to more difficult challenges.

Some changes I need to make in my own life	The obstacles to making these changes	Some ways I could be more helpful in reducing the resistance of others to change

FIFTEEN

CHALLENGING

One of the most effective ways to overcome resistance is to challenge a belief or behavior. Deb wanted to talk about Number 11, "My self-worth is...." She was working hard at just trying to feel good about herself and her personal growth. After we had talked for a while, I responded:

PW23: What you're talking about is growth, and the question that I would have is, "Is there any healing that needs to take place before growth can come?" Maybe you don't have enough energy right now for both....

PW23: People need permission to take time to heal when that is necessary. Animals take time out from their activities to lick their wounds. The use of the word healing *can at times be therapeutic and freeing because it is a word of hope. There are some experiences, such as the ones Deb tells about in D24, for which healing is the only remedy.*

D24: Yep. There probably is. I probably haven't allowed myself the time it takes. I want it now. And I don't really know what the healing would be. I've gone through most of it, I think.... *[Pause]* I got a divorce in October, graduated from college in May, and I got involved in another relationship that ended in June.... I think I'm coming out at the other side, but maybe it's still going to take a little more time....

PW24: I feel like I can be straight and honest with you, just as you have been with me. There's an old saying that "if you crawl from one nest to another, you will never learn to fly." Do you feel like you've learned to "fly" and make it on your own without a man?

PW24: If I feel like my challenge is a fairly strong one, such as the one I use in this response, I often preface it with a remark such as the one in my first sentence of the response.

D25: No, and I agree with that totally, and that's one of the reasons why I've given myself two years. I will not get involved in a heavy relationship for two years, but the need's still there. I still want to.

D25: There is still a "drivenness" with Deb because of the deep need she speaks of.

PW25: So the commitment you've made to yourself has some pain to it. You know you have this need, but it's something that you're willing to pay the price....

D26: Umm-mmmm.... I'm not sure I'm willing to pay the price, because I don't want all the pain that goes along with it.... *[Pause]* But in a relationship I feel like it's really easy for me, out of fear of being rejected, to just not say anything bad, so nobody ever hears what I feel is wrong about things in the relationship.

PW26: So you get used.

D27: Yeah, because I don't assert myself.

PW27: And you're afraid to voice this or assert yourself because...?

D28: Then they'll leave.

PW28: So, part of what you're dealing with is the fear of abandonment. It's a big fear. How old were you when you first felt it?

PW28: Deb has been paying a big price because of her fear of abandonment.

D29: Five.

At that point we began talking about the rejection she experienced when she was five years old, and the need she has felt since that time always to have someone "strong" to take care of her.

Deb's resistance to change was very deep—the stark terror of feeling like an abandoned child in a world of giants. I do not think we would have identified this resistance nearly as rapidly if I had not challenged her behavior of going from one man to another, by use of the crawling-from-one-nest-to-another metaphor. When challenging, it is most important to avoid offending or humiliating. Challenging can only be done effectively when a mutual feeling of respect exists between the people involved.

Deb and I continued to talk:

PW32: When you've attached yourself to a man, or he's attached himself to you, did you put that person in the father or parent image?

D33: I did that with my ex-husband. I don't want to do that anymore. *[Pause]*

PW33: In the past you let yourself be used rather than face the terror of rejection, and in the process I think you've lost some self-respect.

PW33: People gain strength when they get their integrity back. On the other hand, there is a loss of energy that goes with the draining of self-respect.

D34: Yeah, I think so, too. *[Pause]*

PW34: Do you sense that you're impulsive; is that any part of where you are?

D35: Yeah.

PW35: So that would make it hard to trust yourself if you sometimes feel like a car on ice, sliding without being able to direct it. When you violate your conscience—I'm not talking about society's conscience, or mine—but when you violate your conscience, has that been a way you've lost self-respect?

PW35: Another way that Deb will gain personal strength will be to be able to trust herself again. If she cannot trust herself, she is at the mercy of others.

D36: Yeah, I think I've begun to realize that. You know, before, I don't think that I even knew that I was doing that, but now I call it "listening to myself," and I've found that if I listen to myself, things always turn out better...but yet I still refuse to sometimes.

D36: Deb was finding a new way to make decisions—listening to herself.

We talked a bit more about the importance of listening to oneself. I told her the strengths I saw in her, and we began to draw the conversation to a close. We had talked earlier in the conversation about spiritual resources. She said she "quit hearing the voices of organized religion" some time ago, but that she did believe in God.

PW38: Well, we've worked quite a while.... As we are winding down now, are there things that stand out in the conversation?

PW38: By asking an open-ended question like this at the end of our conversation, we can get feedback about what was most useful in our responses, as well as help the other person focus on one or two things to take away.

D39: I'm feeling a lot stronger...that what I've been telling myself all this time is true, and I can trust myself now.

PW39: Where's that coming from?

D40: Inside.

PW40: Is there any other thing that you're seeing differently after our time together?

D41: I'm less desperate.

PW41: That's interesting because I would guess that when you've been desperate, you've done rash things. ... So maybe our time together helped you to listen to yourself, and if that happened I'm excited about that because I think you are worth listening to!

D42: I hope so.

As the above verbatims show, I continued to be fairly confrontational with Deb throughout the conversation. I felt the relationship we established early in the exchange was strong enough to allow her to handle the challenges. She is very motivated to work on her healing and growth, and it is this motivation that enables her to benefit from challenges.

CHALLENGING OTHERS TO GROW

We have been looking at how challenging can be used to release healing. It can also be used to promote growth. Pat was a man who believed that he might lose his wife to another man, and he had thus battled jealousy for a long time. As nearly as I could determine, his wife had given him no reason to believe she was looking elsewhere for affection. However, she was about "fed up" with his jealous behavior.

I tried to figure out how to challenge his belief that his "hanging on tight" would keep her from leaving. So I made a tight fist with my hand and asked Pat what happens when we hold on to people too tightly. He said that we would either suffocate them or cause them to try to get away. He added that his wife at times told him she felt suffocated, and that if he didn't get rid of his jealousy, she was going to leave him.

I told him about the anniversary card my wife gave me a number of years ago, which said: "We cannot OWN each other. We cannot CHANGE each other. We can only DISCOVER each other." If I had only succeeded in challenging Pat's beliefs about "possessing" his wife, that would not have been enough. We have to know, not only what *not* to do, but also what *to do*. So I challenged him to take a new look at his marriage relationship, in fact, at all of his relationships, through discovering eyes. The human personality cannot be discovered even in a full lifetime of effort. But what we do discover can make the effort worthwhile! Discovery as a way of life can be freeing to the person we discover, and to ourselves!

THE "MUM EFFECT"

Gerard Egan's book, *The Skilled Helper,* is filled with useful suggestions for skill building, including specific ideas for effective challenging. He discusses the victims of the "mum effect"—"which refers to people's tendency to withhold bad news from others even when they know it is in others' interest to hear this news."

Egan points out: "In ancient times the person who bore bad news to the king was sometimes killed. This obviously led to a certain reluctance on the part of messengers to bring such news."[1]

A challenge to another person should be a gift of love, free from any need to punish or "straighten out." Other people typically will not respond constructively unless they "hear" our caring. But if we can challenge in an effective, loving way, we can help a friend take some big steps toward healing and growth. Among Egan's principles for effective challenging are:

Earning the right to challenge.
Being concrete and specific.
Challenging clients to clarify values.
Remaining positive.

LIFE-LAB

In terms of challenging, you may be "bland," very reluctant to confront. Or you may be "sharp," eager to challenge, even if it is not always good for the other person. This week, try adjusting your input to your friend's conversational diet so that you use just the appropriate amount of "salt." Since the people you encounter will have different tastes, some will require more or less salt than others. The general guideline in helping is that we need to "discover" other persons and thereby learn how to help them. It may be useful to reread chapter three, "Individualizing," this time with challenging in mind.

SIXTEEN

RESOLVING AND MEDIATING CONFLICTS

Nurses are called on nearly every day to *resolve* a conflict between themselves and another staff member or a patient, or to *mediate* a conflict between two persons. Because of all this practice, many nurses are highly skilled in dealing with conflicts. I have learned how to deal more effectively with conflict from nurses such as the one who tells the story below. She mediated a long-standing conflict between an adult daughter and her dying father in such a way that the two were reconciled:

Brenda came into the office and asked what Hospice could do for her father. She talked in detail about her ninety-seven-year-old father, who had lived in a nursing home for several years. She, an only child, lived out of state. Brenda asked her father's physician not to perform any extraordinary measures to keep her father alive and he agreed. Her father had said that he had prayed for and desired to die.

Although she had decided not to do extraordinary procedures, I asked her how she felt about that decision. She replied that she was comfortable with the decision, and I felt that her conversation indicated that she was.

Arrangements were made for her father to be transferred to a step-down care facility. Several days later I saw her in the cafeteria. She said that her father was not lacking in physical care, but she felt uneasy about the personal relationship that existed between the two of them. I asked her to clarify that for me. She related that they had had many disagreements and could only tolerate each other's company for short periods of time. She said that talking about daily happenings was easy but she found it difficult to talk to him about her feeling for him as her father. I asked, "Do you mean you find it difficult to tell him you care for him?"

She replied, "Yes, but I know he knows how I feel."

I asked, "Are you sure? It sounds like you would really like to tell your father how you feel about him but find it awkward." She nodded agreement, and I went on, "Sometimes it helps to start with, 'I know we haven't always agreed on things, but I want to say thank you for being my father.'" A few more minutes passed, and Brenda said she had to return to the nursing home because she told her father she would only be gone a short time.

About a week later I received a phone call from her. She was catching a noon flight home, but she wanted to tell me that she had gone back to the nursing home the day we had talked to sit beside her father. That afternoon they moved her father's roommate to another room. She sat beside the bed thinking of what we had talked about. She said she reached out and held her father's hand and began to talk, using my words—"We haven't always agreed on things, but I want to say thank you for being my father." She said that once she had started, the words had flowed freely and she was able to tell him all the things that she had wished before that she could talk to him about. Her father was not able to talk, but she was sure he looked at her and said, "Really." He died the next day. She said that she felt at peace, having been able to share with him her love for him.

Peacemaking! That is the goal of conflict resolution and mediation. How do you increase these skills? An effective way is to *begin where you are*—with your present conflict-resolution style. You have a personal style in everything you do. You have a style of walking that is uniquely yours, so that your family and friends can recognize you from a long way off by the way you walk. You have a unique style of learning and integrate your logic and intuition in a special way. You also integrate seeing, hearing, touching, and moving in a way that no one else does. In addition, you have a unique style of responding, with a special blend of senses, emotions, thoughts, choices, and action. Finally, you have a style of resolving conflicts that is not quite like that of anyone else. Have you thought about your style of conflict resolution?

SOME DIFFERENT STYLES OF COPING WITH CONFLICT

I have asked hundreds of people to describe their style of interacting in conflict situations. Most had never tried to do this. Some said they had one style of resolving conflicts with a family member, another style with a close friend, and still another with their boss. While it is true that we handle conflicts with different people in a somewhat different way, I believe that elements of our style show up in nearly all our disagreements and conflicts.

Most of us have a style that is consistently closer to "fight" on the one hand, or "flight" on the other. Neither fight nor flight works well, but they are both used often. Here is how one "fighter" described her approach to settling a conflict:

I am definitely a fighter! When I get into a fight, I yell a lot. My whole family were yellers, and I started to become a yeller during my sophomore year in high school. I have trouble expressing myself to others and I get so frustrated, I yell.

While some people habitually come into conflict leading with their left, others back off from conflicts or, in some cases, run away:

The way I approach conflict is by staying quiet. Often I've tried to explain my position but I never say the right thing so I just keep quiet. I would really like to know when and what to say that would work.

Another flight person said:

My conflict-resolution style is to run. It is easier for me to leave and get things straightened out in my mind, and then go talk with the person involved. My folks resolved their conflicts by arguing the point, then not talking to each other. This silence would go on until one would break down and give in to the other. This is also how the sibling conflicts were handled. I handle conflicts with my friends by leaving. If the person feels close to me or I to them, I will go back and talk with them. Those that are not close to me, I let them drift away.

Here is an example that combined fight and flight:

As a child I witnessed my parents solve conflicts by "having it out" in words, departing mad, and not speaking for a period of time. Their resolution with my brother and me tended to be to point out the error of our ways and punish accordingly, although my brother got more physical punishment and I got reasons and explanations. My brother and I settled our differences through getting-the-last-word, "whispering" matches, and unobtrusive jabs whenever and wherever possible. My friends and I more often than not disagreed, "had it out" verbally and occasionally physically, cooled off, talked, and resumed the friendship.

As a result of, or in spite of, these early childhood experiences, I tend to be a person who dislikes conflict and yet has a boiling point. Most of my difficulty in conflict resolution is related directly to physical or mental fatigue. At those times I tend to blow or cry. Otherwise I tend to reason, discuss, and seek a solution so everyone saves face. I absolutely refuse to let things go for any long period of time in quiet hatred, and I will point out the error of my ways first just to get things back on the road to recovery.

As we have seen, people's style of conflict resolution differs in terms of their preference for fight or flight. It also differs in the time-interval dimension. Some report that they cannot (or will not) talk about the disagreement at the moment of the conflict. Others report that they "have to talk about it right now." My experience with couples is that these two extremes generally marry each other! Perhaps God, acting out of a knowledge that one of the biggest enemies of intimacy in marriage is boredom, has arranged it so that these couples would not be bored. At any rate, the time-interval dimension ("now" or "later") is an important one to be sensitive to in a conflict.

DISCOVERING YOUR CONFLICT-RESOLUTION STYLE
Someone has noted that "fish discover water last," which suggests, in this case, that those around you have been aware of your conflict-resolution style for a long time. Therefore, one way to learn more about your approach to conflict is to ask two or three people who are very close to you to describe how you respond to conflict. Try to listen carefully, keep your defenses down, and look for emerging patterns.

If, on the other hand, you prefer to look within rather than to ask others, you may follow the plan below:

1. Think about your family of origin (your growing-up family—parents and siblings).

How did your parents settle their disagreements and conflicts with each other?

How did your parents settle disagreements with their children and, later, with their teens?

How did the siblings, including you, settle differences with each other, particularly as you got older?

How about your extended family—grandparents, aunts and uncles, and so on?

Was there a common approach to conflict taken by most of your family members?

Are you able to see how your own conflict-resolution style

began to emerge? Did you take any family member as a model in this area?

2. Think about a few of the hundreds of conflicts you saw as you went through elementary school, junior high school, and senior high school—teachers with students, students with students, and perhaps teachers with teachers. Administrators and parents may have been part of some of the scenes. What conclusions did you come to as you observed power struggles? Who usually started the power struggles? Who usually won? Is "power struggle" a part of your method of conflict resolution?

3. Think back to your friendships—boyfriends or girlfriends, or just friends. When a friendship was ending, what did you do? What did you do when you found distance growing between you and your best friend?

4. On the basis of the above reflections, write a paragraph describing your usual style of resolving conflicts. Here is a paragraph that one person wrote:

I've never evaluated myself on my conflict-resolution skills. I generally tuck away any anger underneath a calm submissive blanket. Lately though in my job as a resident assistant in a college resident hall, I've had to deal with other people's conflicts. This has seemed easier for me. I help them slow down, look at what is the problem between them, and work on one problem at a time. We search out several alternative solutions and make a plan to deal with the issue differently next time— a corrective plan of change.

5. After you have written your paragraph, ask a couple of friends or family members to read and verify or challenge your observations.

6. Once you are satisfied that this paragraph describes accurately your style of working with conflicts, go over it again and place a *K* by those things you want to keep, and a *C* by those things you want to change.

7. Now you have identified a factor or two in your style you want to change. How will you make this change?

8. Any factor in a "style" is very difficult to change. An

effective method for me has been to find a mentor, that is, someone who is functioning at a high level in this factor, and who will agree to serve not only as a model but also as a teacher as I try to implement this new element in the way I live.

EXAMINING THE CONFLICT-RESOLUTION STYLE OF JESUS
Another method I have used to learn how to change my conflict-resolution style was to do a study of the life of Christ, looking at that quality, characteristic, or behavior I am seeking to add to my life. Whether it has been gentleness, touch, or firmness, I have always been helped by such a study. One way to do a study of Jesus' style of resolving conflicts is to read Luke 9, which has in it a number of conflict situations, including:

1. A disagreement with the disciples as to whether to send a huge crowd away without any food, or find some way to feed them (verses 10-17).

2. The need to mediate an argument among the disciples as to which of them was the greatest (verses 46-48).

3. A disagreement between Jesus and the disciples concerning what to do with a man who was driving demons out of people, but who did not belong to the disciples' group (verses 49-50).

4. A disagreement between Jesus and some of the disciples about what to do with a village that would not receive them for the night. James and John (the "sons of thunder") were offended and wanted to call fire down from heaven and destroy the town and its people (verses 51-56).

5. Jesus pointed out to several would-be followers how difficult discipleship would be (verses 57-62).

As you read and reread Luke 9, think about these questions:

How is caring shown to be a first principle in Jesus' conflict-resolution style?

How did Jesus mediate the issue of comparative greatness

among the disciples in such a way that they were humbled but not humiliated?

What did Jesus have to say about the spirit of exclusiveness ("He's not a member of our group")?

How did Jesus respond to the revenge motive that was pushing some of his disciples toward violence when they were refused hospitality by the people of the Samaritan village?

RESOLVING A CONFLICT WITH A FRIEND OR FAMILY MEMBER

Once you have discovered your own conflict-resolution style and have begun to target parts of it for change, if needed, you are ready to start applying this skill with others. Conflict *resolution* occurs when you find a mutually acceptable way to meet the needs of another person and yourself. Conflict *mediation* differs in that you are working in this instance to help two other people resolve their differences. We will work first with conflict resolution and then with conflict mediation.

With the publication of *Getting to Yes,* by Roger Fisher and William Ury, there is now available a brief reference book on effectively resolving and mediating conflicts.[1] The main points made in the book are that conflicts should be handled according to a moral principle—both persons or "sides" must benefit; and the persons involved should not take a position (if you...then I...), but should actively seek the best interests of all involved and should creatively invent options that meet these interests. These ideas are not new, but they are put together in an especially helpful way.

Some other tested guidelines for resolving conflicts are:

1. *Try not to corner the other person.* People who feel cornered will often use a fight-flight reaction. If there is room, they will run away—one person by saying, "I didn't do it," and another by refusing to talk. If there is no room to get away, they will fight, by arguing, yelling, or sometimes even hitting. You give the other person "psychological room" by

talking calmly, listening accurately, and responding gently but firmly.

2. *Adopt the rule, "Don't back down, give up, or attack."* It is important that you do nothing that will diminish or put down the other person, such as yelling or using sarcasm. It is also important that you not allow another person to diminish or intimidate you. This latter goal can be accomplished by standing erect, using direct eye contact (rather than looking down), and responding honestly.

3. *Adopt an attitude of hope* —one that says, "We can work it out." This positive stance will be very useful in resolving the conflict.

4. *Let your friend know the things you appreciate about him or her, as well as the things with which you are in disagreement.*

5. *Respond briefly each time you say something.* In chapter thirty of *How to Help a Friend*, "The Brief Response," some evidences are given that show a brief response is more effective than a long one.

6. *Set a follow-up time for a week or two later.* Plan to get together again to see if the conflict is resolved or if progress is being made on it. Keep circling back until the situation is resolved.[2]

MEDIATING A CONFLICT

Peacemaking is risky. The two people you are trying to get to work together may both get angry at you, the mediator. We all know what may happen when someone gets in the middle of a lovers' quarrel. The most dreaded call for many police officers is a family disturbance.

I have been asked to mediate conflicts in several organizational settings. One of the most successful efforts was one in which I chose not to get directly involved. A church board chairman called me for that purpose. There were two factions that had polarized the church. Since I was too busy to go, I recommended a professional conflict mediator. When he told them his fee would be $1,500, the chairman said that would cause a bigger conflict than it would resolve! Armed with this sobering information, the chairman went back to the warring factions, which found a way to patch up their differences. There is nothing like an external threat to bring about internal closeness!

As a mediator, your first task will often be to deal with hurt and anger. Usually by the time a friend, fellow worker, or church member gets involved with two disagreeing people, one or both have already been humiliated. Nothing of a rational nature can be done until this is handled. One of the most effective ways of achieving this is to try to bring out the pain with a question such as "Where is the hurting for you in all this?" The pain is the first emotion, whereas anger springs from that pain. People will usually continue to hurt back and seek revenge until their own pain is expressed.

In most conflicts both persons have already taken a position. A supervisor may say, "If he does that once more, I'm going to fire him." The supervisor has taken a stand and thereby made mediation impossible. As Fisher and Ury point out, it is much more effective to find out the interests of both sides without first becoming entrenched in positions. Is there a way to meet the interests of *both* persons? That is what conflict mediation is all about.

As a friend of a couple or a family, you may find yourself challenged as a peacemaker. Family members can be particularly vicious with each other because of the deep emotions involved and their long-shared history, some of which has been abrasive. There are times in families when "negotiation" does not work. The only things that work then are spiritual resources, especially forgiveness. I have a sign in my counseling office that says, "To err is human, to forgive is—out of the question!" This is an effort to nudge people to consider forgiveness as a creative alternative. As you model the love of Christ in relating to both individuals, you may be able to touch them with that love and thereby release forgiveness. Once you do this, mediation will then become possible.

Richard C. Halverson has discussed in a very helpful way how Jesus is the model in our peacemaking:

Good relationships come through love and forgiveness... *somebody has to be vulnerable—to lead from weakness—to give in—to lose....*

Good relationships are not based on the 50/50 principle....

Someone has to be willing to go all the way... *all the time....*

Love and forgiveness are costly...but they are the price of good relationships....

Which is why it is so easy to talk peace...*so costly to have it.*

Peace talkers are a dime a dozen... peacemakers are rare and priceless.

Jesus Christ is the perfect model. He never negotiated... He loved—He gave and gave and gave...*all the way to the cross!*

Relationship begins when somebody leads from weakness!

"If God so loved us, we ought to love one another."
I John 4:11.[3]

LIFE-LAB

This is a skill for which I genuinely hope you will have no practice experiences. You certainly should not seek out conflicts to resolve or mediate, unless you are distanced with a friend or a family member and know that you will have to deal with a conflict situation before you can again become close. Sometimes two old friends, or spouses, or brothers and sisters neglect their friendship. Often, one of them will "pick a fight," because people have to get close to fight. I am convinced that this is sometimes done without the persons involved knowing why they are fighting. Many times, one of the participants will say, "What we are fighting about doesn't amount to anything." In these situations we need to work at restoring the relationship rather than arbitrating the trivial disagreement.

When you do get the opportunity to resolve or mediate a conflict, the best way to relive the conversation later is by getting feedback from the other participant(s) involved. What did you do or say that worked? At what point in the conversation did the other person(s) feel for the first time they were moving closer rather than further away? This feedback will help you to increase your peacemaking skills.

We begin life in a small group—our family. Small, caring groups recapitulate the family and thus have a great deal of power in the areas of personal healing and growth. Because of this primal power of small groups, they may also do harm. Therefore, goodwill and group leadership skills are two essential components of working with a small group. The group leader, often an emergent or informal coordinator rather than an officially designated chairperson, can work to assure that healing and growth are possible and that the potential for harm is minimized. The leader can also help the group become an avenue of personal renewal for its members.

The topics covered in this section include:

*Developing a Releasing Style
of Group Leadership
Creating and Nourishing a
Renewal-Support-Training
Group*

P A R T 6

HEALING AND GROWTH IN SMALL GROUPS

DEVELOPING A RELEASING STYLE OF GROUP LEADERSHIP

After graduating from college, I went back to graduate school whenever I had a major question that I could not get answered otherwise. The first question-asking trip was to theological seminary to grow in my own personal faith and biblical knowledge. An incident that symbolized my reasons for going to seminary was that I had killed an ant. A fellow Christian who witnessed this act told me I was not supposed to kill anything and offered as proof Exodus 20:14, "Thou shalt not kill" (King James Version). Well, I didn't think that had to do with killing ants, but I wasn't sure. I decided that if I did not prepare myself for answering theological questions, I would be at the mercy of others all my life. So I went off to seminary for three years and learned, among other things, that Exodus 20:14 has to do with committing *murder* of human beings.

After leaving seminary, I began teaching English in high school. It was enjoyable, but a new puzzlement began to nag at me. Students came by individually to talk, and I found myself counseling—and not knowing what I was doing. So I went back for another degree, this time in counseling, and later changed careers from teaching to counseling. Then I found to my dismay that students came for counseling not only individually, but also in groups of two, three, or more. Once more I trudged back to school, this time to work three years on my last (I hope) degree, with the major part of my study being in group counseling.

I wanted to learn how to lead a small group of people effectively so that healing and growth could be released. As I learned some things about small group leadership skills, I came to appreciate even more the difficulty of leading a group. There are unseen forces working that are much more powerful than any influence we can bring to bear.

THE POWER OF GROUPS

The family unit, work clusters, coffee gatherings, tennis doubles, small church committees, and other groups that we are in influence our lives in many ways. Groups tend to generate their own pressures once they become close. For example, many churches pressure their members to conform. These promptings come in unseen, subtle ways, not by statements in the constitution and by-laws. Everybody heeds the unwritten pressures to conform, while not everybody reads the by-laws.

Some small groups have a great deal of power. So what? The "so what?" is that the number-one rule for a small-group leader should be: "Do no harm." The leader of a group needs to see to it that no member of the group is ever diminished by other members. Also, if someone wants to share a personal matter in a group, the motivation should come from within that person. It should not result from a pressure to share because other group members did. On the other hand, group pressures can be beneficial. One such influence can be an unwritten rule that might go something like this, "We will protect the integrity of each group member and help each one work towards wellness."

GROUP LEADERSHIP—DESIGNATED AND EMERGENT

You may not see yourself as a group leader. Chances are you

lead many groups each month. You may have been designated a leader—a mother or father, charge nurse, teacher, or committee chairperson. Or you may emerge as the leader within a group, whether or not the group has a specified leader. There are many times within work groups or committees that one person is tacitly given the leadership role by the other members.

The latter situation often occurs when an informal group meets without a designated leader. A group gets together to talk each day at a work break; friends meet at a restaurant, or an informal "leaderless" Bible study gathers regularly or intermittently. In each of these and other informal settings, there is usually a leader, although probably no one talks about this. Sometimes the same person is the leader each time. In other groups, different persons may be given the group leadership at different times. In a car pool, the driver is often the leader, and the person who does not want to be involved (or wants to sleep!) may sit in the rear seat directly behind the driver. Incidentally, it is not always the person who talks the most who is given the role of leader. More often it is the one whom the members see as best able to meet the needs of the group who earns the right to lead, whether or not he/she desires that leadership.

WHAT MAKES A GROUP?
Cohesiveness is the word given to the factor that differentiates between a collection of people and a group. A gathering of people may occur for months or even years without ever becoming a group—note some committees, church school classes, and even families—while other gatherings become cohesive in five minutes.

How can you assist a gathering of people to become cohesive, and therefore a group? The effective leader is responsive to members' needs. A group becomes cohesive rapidly if the members perceive that it can serve as a vehicle to meet their needs. Therefore, in the groups to which you belong, listen to the yearnings, spoken and unspoken, of the other members. Complaints and negativisms may be caused not only by real environmental situations, but also by a perceived lack of personal significance and meaning. You can be the catalyst for helping the group discover how it can help members meet these deep spiritual needs. For example, members of one small "leaderless" support group felt the need to center their lives—to live by new priorities. The informal leader suggested a study of the life of Christ. The group then chose the Gospel of Mark and studied it over a long period of time.

Another example is the college department in which I work. The faculty members began to feel a hunger to do more in the weekly departmental meetings than take care of the necessary tasks on the agenda. Through the work of designated and emergent leaders, we have now moved to a new format in our department meetings. We typically take the first fifteen minutes to celebrate an event in one or more of the ten faculty members' lives. A family member made a volleyball team, a child was born, an anniversary was observed, a dream was realized—we have found scores of events worthy of celebration. And no one should have to celebrate alone. This new format has had interesting fringe benefits. We have cut our departmental meeting time by about 35 percent. The celebration is probably not the sole cause, but I'm sure it's one of them. When a group takes time to recognize and affirm its members, it is able to accomplish its tasks more efficiently.

Another method that helps build cohesiveness in a group is for the leader to work toward releasing each member to talk. When the leader or one group member talks at length, the cohesiveness of the group usually declines. The New Testament evidences indicate that in our Lord's small group (the twelve disciples), Jesus did not do all the talking. The members asked questions, protested, made comments, and argued, and all these interchanges were grist for the mill that produced spiritual growth.

You, of course, can control the length of your own responses. But how about a "long talker" within the group—
the one who, when he/she begins to talk, may not observe
the other group members begin to recline in their chairs?
Often, people who talk a long time do so in order to be understood. They usually thus guarantee that they are not understood, since others "turn them off." When they sense they
are not being understood, they keep on talking. Therefore, it
is often helpful if you let this member know you are understanding what he/she is saying. If that fails, use the resources
of the group. If there is a monopolizer in the group, the
other members are permitting this, maybe even encouraging
it. Work to give the silent members "permission" to talk,
with a statement such as "Jane, you look as if this discussion
has triggered some deep thinking. I believe the group would
benefit by hearing your reactions, if you'd be willing to share
them." It is important to lead from the "center" rather than
the "front," that is, utilize all the resources and wisdom of
the group.

GIVING AND RECEIVING IN A GROUP
One of the reasons a group is so therapeutic is that we can
both give and receive in that setting. We give when we offer
another group member our time and attention in a loving
way. We receive when other group members offer us their
love. Some people are great at giving and poor at receiving.
This is sometimes true of those who work in the human services, for example, counseling, teaching, nursing, and pastor-
ing. On the other hand, there are those who are excellent at
receiving (taking) but not good at giving. People who see
only their own needs fit this category. Others may be effective
at both giving and receiving, while still others are frightened
of groups and scared to try either giving or receiving.

The most effective way to involve "shy" group members is
to make the group setting a safe one. Perhaps you teach an

adult class in church school. You want an atmosphere that is relational. One of the keys to this kind of class is to work toward a cooperative rather than a competitive climate. When someone in the class says something, try as often as you can to build on that person's remark as you expand an idea or go on to the next idea or topic. You can do this by saying, "The point you just made, Bill, lets me see this passage in a new way." Or, "The point Bill just made serves as an excellent base for the next topic we'll be considering." By doing this, you will help members begin to realize that they are all making a valuable contribution. Be patient with yourself as the leader. Establishing a noncompetitive, mutually supportive climate is not easy. Even the group in which our Lord was the leader had trouble with competitiveness—". . . they had been arguing among themselves about who was the greatest" (Mark 9:34b).

SOME DIFFERENCES IN INDIVIDUAL AND GROUP COUNSELING
You can apply nearly all the counseling and helping skills taught in this book in a group setting as well as in a one-to-one relationship. But group work does involve some additional skills. The leader needs to "monitor" the rest of the group occasionally, instead of focusing only on the one who is talking. A guideline can be that "the one who makes the investment gets the interest." Sometimes you may notice that another member is making a bigger emotional investment than the one who is talking. Such involvement may be signaled by a pained expression or eyes that have filled with tears. That member should have the next opportunity to respond. The opportunity can be given by your saying, "Joan, you looked as if you had a concern. Is this something you want to mention here?" Thus, as a leader you have given permission or encouragement to respond, but you have not required her to do so.

Another responsibility one has as a group leader that is different from what exists in a one-to-one situation is that the leader is responsible for protecting the one making the emotional investment from being harmed by others. Because people are especially vulnerable when they are sharing pain, they are more open to injury. To be consistent with the guideline of "Do no harm," the leader may need to intervene if another member starts giving cheap advice, thereby showing he/she has not really understood the pain of the person talking or is uncomfortable with the other's expression of pain. The intervention can be a gentle one, such as, "Before we work on a solution for Joan, could we take some more time, just to be sure we're all with her in what she's going through right now."

RELEASING INSTEAD OF CONTROLLING

Can an effective group leader be likened to a coach, an orchestra conductor, or a choreographer? Probably all of these direct and control more than a group leader should. Yet an effective coach, conductor, or choreographer all release the people they work with to play or dance well. It is this releasing aspect that is a part of all effective group leaders. They free the group to become all that it can be—so that its members are released to become all they can be.

LIFE-LAB

Think through, or jot down, the different small groups you will spend time with this week. When I did this just now, I jotted down eleven groups on my first consideration of the week—family group, work groups, church groups, and others. Are you the designated leader in any of them? An emergent leader? How can you help group members be more cooperative with each other rather than competitive? How can you interact with the quiet members of each group to draw out their resources? How can you be a releasing force within the groups, so as to help members be accepted and move toward healing and growth?

A releasing style of group leadership requires one to be very active in terms of awareness and interventions. One of the most useful things you can do is to *involve* yourself with as many of the group members as possible by investing time in them, discovering their interests, and showing you care. In the next chapter, which is also the last, I will be introducing a special group that in many ways can serve as a model for our participation in all other groups.

EIGHTEEN

CREATING AND NOURISHING A RENEWAL-SUPPORT-TRAINING GROUP

About five years ago I started meeting with two other men for Bible study, usually weekly. We have continued to meet during these years, but not always regularly. We have broadened our purposes for meeting. Sometimes we have breakfast together. We have prayed together. We have met together to talk about our predicaments and, in some cases, our crises. Two of us accompanied the third man to the town where he grew up, to be with him at the funeral of his mother. Not always do all three of us meet; sometimes just two of us get together. Yet, I think we all three feel a special kinship and bond with the other two. It is the spiritual bond of being brothers in Christ.

RENEWAL. Our group meets a number of needs. The need for renewal is a recurring one in most of our lives. As winter comes to us in one form or another, it calls for spring. We experience burnout, stress, disappointment, failure, grief, or anxiety, and find that we cannot make it back to wholeness by ourselves. Many people have a family group that is central in providing ongoing renewal. But a renewal group outside the family can help us give more to the family and not just receive from it. So, for me, renewal is a vital part of my small group.

SUPPORT. The group has also supported me at times in my life when I have especially needed that support. This differs from renewal, which involves a periodic need to be restored after a traumatic event, or after a gradual deterioration has left us somewhat "deadened." We are, in a sense, brought back to life by the renewal process. Support has some of the same life-giving qualities as renewal. But instead of being periodic in nature, support is constant and sustaining. I feel supported when I know that others are thinking about me, caring about me, and lifting a prayer for me. Even when they are not with me, Bud and Kent provide unseen support for the living and venturing I do every day. There have been many tangible evidences of that support—a phone call just to see how I'm doing, a hug when I've needed it, a note, an affirmation, a push to get my regular medical examination done, a gift, or other expression of love. I don't know what I would have done the last five years without this support.

TRAINING. I have come to believe that the training aspect of a small group is very important. Specifically, I believe that the training needs to promote spiritual growth. When I look back on the life of our group, some of the most inspiring times have been our Bible studies. We spent a year and a half studying the life of Christ in the Gospels. Almost every morning that we met, we left each other with a new insight or commitment. We are now studying together on the topic of prayer, using the Bible and a small study book on that subject. We have already decided that when we end this study, we will begin one on the Holy Spirit.

In a nutshell, the renewal function of the group has meant healing. The support function has provided companionship and courage for daily life and work. The training function has been an avenue for systematic spiritual growth. In the final analysis, if we do not grow spiritually, the other two functions of the group become impossible.

CREATING A ReST GROUP

I do not think that ReST is a totally descriptive acronym for a

Renewal-Support-Training group, but at least it takes up less space than spelling it all out. If you are not now in such a group and would like to start one, you may find the following guidelines useful.

1. In choosing a friend, or friends, to join you, make the primary criterion a spiritual kinship. Nothing else will provide the bond that will meet your deepest needs and allow the group to survive and grow. For me, spiritual kinship means the shared belief that Christ is Lord and that we are brothers and sisters in the family of God.

2. Because the training function of a group enhances the renewal and support functions, consider starting with some training project that has the potential to contribute to your spiritual growth. For example, share with the other(s) in your group some Bible study topics, or some books of the Bible, that you have wanted to know more about for a long time. Get the other group members' ideas, come to a consensus for your first study, and begin.

3. You may begin with one or more friends. The more of you there are, the more difficult it will be to find meeting times. If you start with just one other person, it will be necessary for both of you to have an equal part in the choice of a third person, if and when you decide to expand your group.

MAINTAINING THE GROUP

The shared meeting time will probably be insufficient to keep the group alive. The group members will also need to touch base with each other individually during the week by seeing each other, by a phone call, or through another kind of contact. Sometimes this is difficult, given the rapid pace and different schedules of several people. The more people there are in the group, the more difficult it is. But, generally speaking, if we care for each other during the group meeting once a week, we will find a way of caring for each other during the week.

Our own ReST group has discovered that when we have
neglected our Bible study, we have ceased to meet regularly.
The Bible study offers a purpose beyond ourselves that serves
as a magnet to bring us together. I saw a poster once that
read, "There is one among you whom you do not recognize."
In a way, our Bible study together has served to recognize
the presence of Christ in our group, as well as meet our need
for spiritual growth.

There have been many reasons not to meet for Bible study.
One of us is out of town, or there is a conflict in schedules,
and we put it off—and put it off. Determination is needed at
this point in order for the group to work.

RELIVING OUR ReST GROUP
Yesterday Bud and Kent and I got together to look back over
the years. Excerpts from this conversation are shown below:

PAUL: I thought that we could just say anything that comes to
our mind about the group. I think we started the group about
five years ago....

KENT: It seems to me it would have been at *least* five
years.... One of the things that comes to my mind is a kind
of sense of freedom or a sense of acceptance, so that I always
felt free to go in whatever direction I needed to go.... When
I feel best in a relationship is when there is a spontaneity,
and for me that has been one of the real neat things about
this. There's been spontaneous laughter, and there's been
spontaneous sharing in terms of hard times....

BUD: The spiritual dimension of our studies has...made possible the conditions that we share right now. I guess what is
most important to me is this dependability that I feel from
you two, knowing where you are and that you're there in my
corner under any conditions. And it's great to not feel de-
meaned or debased in any way from sharing some of my
frailties and many mistakes in judgment and behavior. I'm

able to do that better and better with both of you. It's that firm knowledge that I can freely call on either of you anytime, regardless of the calendar or the clock. That's important to me to have that knowledge. Very important. I guess somehow I think that's going to happen. It's inevitable, I suppose, at some time in the future. It's so much easier to know that you will both be there. . . .

KENT: Like "that base is covered."

BUD: That's a big base. Like first, second, third base, and home all in one.

PAUL: That kind of trust means a lot to me. To know that you can trust us, and I do the same with you. I know that if a dreaded event were to occur, if there was a sudden emergency, I would have no question about calling upon either of you to do whatever needed to be done. And to know that that's available, there's a comfort that I experience. I had never put it together just that way. It makes the good times better to know that the bad times are covered.

KENT: Well, the part that I picked up on in terms of what I think you were saying, Bud, was that there isn't even the slightest thought that anything that I would say would not be acceptable, that there's not even the slightest bit of need to be on guard; it's not there at all.

BUD: This has added greatly to my capacity to love, which I've not been too satisfied with, because I love Barb [Kent's wife] and Lillian [Paul's wife] very much, and I share that with them now when I see them.

PAUL: I think one of the important dimensions that you bring to the group, Bud, is some structure, for example, calling us back to Bible study. I think one of your gifts is organization and taking time out for important things, and that's one thing that has helped keep us functioning as a group. I guess it is dependability.

KENT: I've always admired in you, Bud, just an absolute genuine search, just kind of a continuing exploration to find answers, or to be better. In a sense that's a little bit of a structure, too; it keeps things moving forward.... It's a little like you have been a step or two down the road, searching, journeying, exploring, and so it's been fun for me to follow along. And I have one other thing that I have a strong sense for—every time we get together, I walk away a better person. I just know that! You know, encouraged or empowered or something, where classes and my work at school, and Barb and Erik and Aaron [Kent's two sons, ages six and three], and Kitti and Nikki [his two dogs], and Oscar [the cat] are all better off as a result of this time. *[Laughter]*

PAUL: It seems to me that our getting together has something to do with the rhythm of life. It's like the week is a rhythm, and the day is a rhythm, and the seasons. And there's a comfort knowing that this is one of the beats of life—that I know we're getting together. That's a nice thing about the repetition of good things. It gives a pleasure in the present, a pleasure in memory, and then a delight or anticipation, just as one looks forward to spring.

KENT: I've felt that both of you have taken much, much more responsibility in terms of keeping the group going than I have, and yet you include me and accept me anyway. That's been helpful to me, because at this point either I'm not very good at it or I have a lot of other things going on. And not once have I felt reluctant because I haven't been carrying my weight.

PAUL: ...Bud and I are more in the maintenance stage rather than the creation stage with our families. You are in the creation stage and that takes a lot more time and energy.

BUD: The births in your family, Kent, and the death of your mother have been experiences that have led us closer together....

KENT: For me, it's something as tangible as...I find myself referring to this place [around Bud's dining-room table] because this is almost becoming *the* place right here, but we've met some at your house, Paul, and we've met one time at my house. That just doesn't work very well with Erik and Aaron, but I haven't felt bad in terms of that. I guess it's neat to be in a place where you feel that you are receiving and not feeling, boy, I've got to stay even and pay back.

PAUL: We don't have to be diplomatic with each other.

KENT: I *would* like another piece of toast. *[Laughter]*

KENT: I think another thing that has been important for me is that there has been such a positive sense of humor. We've laughed at so many neat things. I don't remember *what* we laughed at. Certainly what we've done is laugh together, and a lot of it has grown out of laughing at ourselves and sharing that, but it's never seemed to me to be a damaging thing....

PAUL: I think there has been a genuine concern for each other's families.

BUD: That's been very helpful, for me.

KENT: I think that's a really neat point, because I have felt that so strongly from both of you.

THE UNIQUE IMPACT OF SUCH A GROUP

Just as every human being is unique in all the world, so every group is different. Some of the things that have worked in our ReST group will not work in yours. You will learn how to nourish your group by carefully observing and listening to its members.

You will know the group is working if you consistently grow in freedom. As you are more and more released to experience healing and growth in your own life, you can more effectively help others move in the same direction.

THE RELATIONAL LIFE-STYLE

Whether we are in a ReST group or reaching out to help someone who needs us, a crucial element is simply living out the relational life-style. The following story is about someone who did just that. Cathy, who wrote the story, is a sensitive, caring person who was in one of the Counseling Skills classes that Marv Knittel and I teach. She helped create a unique two-person caring group:

One emotion that I find a lot of people have a hard time expressing is that of love. I used to have a real hard time telling people that I loved them. Then my grandma came to live with us because she could no longer care for herself. I grew so close to her in the four years she lived with us. I knew she was dying, just like I knew Grandpa was dying when I was 12. Except this time I wasn't going to sit back and hide the love I felt—that's what I did with Grandpa. I never went to visit him or talk—just to talk. I only told him a few times that I loved him—and even then it was almost under my breath. I was afraid. And I made the decision that I couldn't do that with her. I knew that no matter how many years she had, it would be too few. So I spent every moment I could with her—I shared with her and grew with her—but best of all I really loved her in the true sense of the word "love." And it never was a hidden secret with us. I told her every time I left for school or kissed her good night that I loved her. And it never was hard for me to tell her. I wanted her to know right up to the moment of her death that I loved her and cared. And when she died a part of me died also. But I have peace in knowing that I shared with her and she shared with me some of our innermost thoughts and feelings. She wasn't alone when she died—she had love. And that's all she needed.

I learned and grew so much because of that lady. I don't ever hesitate to tell my mom and dad that I love them. It's easy for me to express my love to my parents and my brothers and sisters—because I don't want to wake up some day and

*find them gone without knowing how much love I feel for
them.*

*Love is a positive emotion, and I wish all people could ex-
press the love they feel for others more openly. It would put
more smiles on people's faces and more laughter in their lives.*

One of the striking features of this story is that it describes
a genuine relationship. It was not just a one-way investment
by Cathy because she wanted to "help" her grandmother.
Cathy said, "I learned and grew so much because of that
lady." The help, the goodness, and the love flowed in both
directions. That is the key to the relational life-style and to
the helping relationship.

As Cathy expressed her love and caring to her grandmother, they were *both* released to share some of their "innermost thoughts and feelings." And Cathy was released
through this experience to express her love comfortably to
her parents and brothers and sisters. Cathy did all this before
she took the Counseling Skills class. She believes, as do Marv
and I, that she is even more effective in helping because of
her work in the class.

I hope that your experience in studying these pages, and
applying them each week in Life-Lab, has helped you also to
become more effective in releasing others and yourself.

APPENDIX A

SUGGESTED READINGS

Carkhuff, Robert R. *The Art of Helping*. 5th ed. Amherst, Mass.: Human Resources Development Press, 1983.

Carkhuff's approach is based on twenty years of research. This is a skill-oriented book that provides the reader with many practice situations.

Collins, Gary R. *Christian Counseling: A Comprehensive Guide*. Waco, Texas: Word Books, 1980.

This is the reading book for the Christian Counselor's Library, a multimedia training resource. The book is probably best used with the Library, an excellent resource that includes a manual, worksheets, and twenty-eight audiocassettes. However, the book also stands by itself and is a truly comprehensive guide.

Combs, Arthur W., and Donald L. Avila. *Helping Relationships: Basic Concepts for the Helping Professions*. 3rd ed. Boston: Allyn and Bacon, 1985.

The aim of this book is to apply concepts of human behavior to the understanding and application of effective helping relationships. The book has an excellent research base, and there are many references for further reading at the end of each chapter.

Crabb, Lawrence J., Jr., and Dan B. Allender. *Encouragement: The Key to Caring.* Grand Rapids: Zondervan Publishing House, 1984.

This is a very useful resource. The authors call encouragement "the most basic form of counseling." They present a number of techniques for encouraging, based on a foundation of Christian principles.

Egan, Gerard. *The Skilled Helper.* 2nd ed. Monterey, Cal.: Brooks/Cole Publishing Co., 1982.

This book provides examples of helping skills across a broad range—all the way from attending to confronting. It provides a thorough, practical approach to developing these skills.

Larson, Bruce. *There's a Lot More to Health Than Not Being Sick.* Waco, Texas: Word Books, 1981.

The biblical perspective in this book provides the direction for moving towards wellness. It can help the reader gain courage to make this move and to help others in a similar quest.

Nickerson, Eileen T., and Kay O'Laughlin, eds. *Helping Through Action: Action-Oriented Therapies.* Amherst, Mass.: Human Resources Development Press, 1982.

Many of the chapters in this book formerly appeared as journal articles. They provide a useful introduction to such action-oriented approaches to helping as games, music, art, and dance.

Peale, Norman Vincent. *The Positive Power of Jesus Christ.* Wheaton, Ill.: Tyndale House Publishers, 1981.

Peale's book not only inspires, but also provides practical helping approaches. The anecdotal approach, the dependence on the Holy Spirit, and the emphasis on hope all give direction to the helper.

Petersen, J. Allan. *The Myth of the Greener Grass.* Wheaton, Ill.: Tyndale House Publishers, 1983.

This is a valuable resource for helpers who want to reach out to married couples involved in the suffering brought on by an extramarital affair. The book provides the knowledge background and the spiritual resources that make intervention possible.

Smedes, Lewis B. *Forgive and Forget.* San Francisco: Harper & Row, 1984.

This has more to do with helping oneself than with helping others. It is included here because forgiveness is so vital to living a released life, and because Smedes writes in a crisp, effective way that gives both personal direction and directions for helping.

Welter, Paul. *How to Help a Friend.* Wheaton, Ill.: Tyndale House Publishers, 1978.

This is a counseling guide for laymen and is designed to help counselors learn to express warmth, identify needs, build on persons' strengths, and respond to crises.

Wilson, Earl D. *Loving Enough to Care.* Portland, Or.: Multnomah Press, 1984.

This biblically-based book reflects Dr. Wilson's lengthy experience in counseling and in training counselors and psychologists. He helps the reader develop caring attitudes and reach out to others.

A CHECKLIST FOR PREFERRED LEARNING CHANNELS

The checklist that follows is adapted from my book *How to Help a Friend.*[1] There is an extensive discussion in that book about preferred learning channels and their relationship to the helping venture.

To use the checklist, read from left to right. Check only one 1 and one 2, and so on. Check the one that is *most descriptive* of you. When you finish, total the checks in each column to get an idea of your strong learning channel (the one with the most checks). Remember that—in terms of accuracy— checklists are somewhere between bathroom scales and tea leaves. But they can be useful in building awareness.

VISUAL	AUDITORY	TOUCH-MOVEMENT
__ 1. Prefers written directions from supervisor	__ 1. Prefers oral directions from supervisor	__ 1. Prefers to "walk through" task with supervisor
__ 2. Likes to use a map to find way in a strange city	__ 2. Likes to ask for directions in a strange city	__ 2. Likes to guess and find own way in a strange city
__ 3. Expresses self best by writing	__ 3. Expresses self best by talking	__ 3. Expresses self best by gestures, art, etc.

___ 4. Prefers reading games, like "Scrabble."

___ 5. Reviews for a test by rereading text and notes

___ 6. Puts model or toy together using written instructions

___ 7. Commits a Zip Code, etc., to memory by rereading it

___ 8. Uses free time for reading

___ 9. Reviews "reminder" lists frequently

___10. Writes a note to congratulate a friend

___11. Usually concentrates deeply on reading material

___12. Observes "body language" closely

___ 4. Prefers talking/listening games

___ 5. Reviews for a test by talking with others or by rereading notes aloud

___ 6. Prefers to have someone else read instructions when assembling something

___ 7. Commits numbers to memory by saying them over and over

___ 8. Uses free time to talk with others

___ 9. Plans the next day or week by talking it through with someone

___10. Calls on telephone or congratulates face-to-face

___11. Usually concentrates deeply on what another person is saying

___12. Listens for voice inflections

___ 4. Prefers movement games

___ 5. Reviews for a test by writing a summary of material to be learned

___ 6. Uses neither written nor oral directions when assembling

___ 7. Commits numbers to memory by writing them again and again

___ 8. Uses free time for physical activities

___ 9. Plans the next day by making a list

___10. Prefers to shake hands, hug, or otherwise get in touch when congratulating

___11. Usually concentrates deeply on a task requiring movement

___12. Likes to touch when communicating

NOTES

INTRODUCTION

1. Bruce Larson, *There's a Lot More to Health Than Not Being Sick* (Waco, Tex.: Word Books, 1981), 24.

CHAPTER 2

1. James Boswell, *The Life of Samuel Johnson,* ed. Frank Brady (New York: Signet Classics, 1968), 109.

CHAPTER 3

1. C. G. Jung, *The Undiscovered Self* (New York: A Mentor Book, New American Library, 1957), 17, 18.

2. M. Scott Peck, *The Road Less Traveled* (New York: Simon & Schuster, 1978), 161.

CHAPTER 6

1. J. Allan Petersen, *The Myth of the Greener Grass* (Wheaton, Ill.: Tyndale House Publishers, 1983).

2. This chart is adapted from Paul Welter, *How to Help a Friend* (Wheaton, Ill.: Tyndale House Publishers, 1978), 94, 95.

CHAPTER 7

1. Viktor Frankl, *Man's Search for Meaning* (Boston: Beacon Press, 1962), 112.

2. Gerald Corey, *Theory and Practice of Counseling and PsychoTherapy,* 2nd ed. (Monterey, Calif.: Brooks/Cole Publishing Co., 1982), 236.

CHAPTER 9

1. Malcolm Knowles, *Self-Directed Learning* (Chicago: Follett Publishing Co., 1975), 15.

CHAPTER 10

1. Walter Wink, *Transforming Bible Study* (Nashville, Tenn.: Abingdon, 1980), 145, 146.
2. From *Guideposts,* vol. 26, no. 15 (April 26, 1984), published by American Association for Counseling and Development, Alexandria, Virginia.
3. Henri J. M. Nouwen, *The Wounded Healer* (Garden City, N.Y.: Image Books, 1979), xvi.
4. Paul Tournier, *The Strong and the Weak* (Philadelphia: The Westminster Press, 1976), 115.

CHAPTER 11

1. Oletta Wald, *The Joy of Discovery in Bible Study,* rev. ed. (Minneapolis: Augsburg Publishing House, 1975).
2. Rick Yohn, *Firsthand Joy* (Colorado Springs: NavPress, 1982).
3. "A Catalog of Bible Study Cassettes for Loan" (Bible Believers Cassettes, Inc., 130 N. Spring St., Springdale, AR 72764).
4. John Claypool, "Primal Healing," *Faith at Work,* March/April 1980, 30.

CHAPTER 12

1. John Naisbitt, *Megatrends* (New York: Warner Books, 1984), 215.

CHAPTER 13

1. Bruno Bettelheim, *The Uses of Enchantment* (New York: Vintage Books, 1977), 25.

CHAPTER 14

1. Sid Simon, workshop in Kearney, Nebraska, November 22–23, 1980.

CHAPTER 15

1. Gerard Egan, *The Skilled Helper* (Monterey, Calif.: Brooks/Cole Publishing Co., 1982), 179.

CHAPTER 16

1. Roger Fisher and William Ury, *Getting to Yes* (New York: Penguin, 1983).
2. Adapted from Paul Welter, *The Nursing Home: A Caring Community* (Valley Forge, Penn.: Judson Press, 1981), 62–66. Used by permission.
3. Richard C. Halverson, from "Perspective," published by Concern Ministries, Inc., McLean, VA 22101, vol. XXXIII, no. 14 (August 5, 1981).

APPENDIX B

1. Paul Welter, *How to Help a Friend* (Wheaton, Ill.: Tyndale House Publishers, 1978), 191.

INDEX

accountability to others, 24, 72, 170
affirmation, 30, 104-106
alienation, 32
anger, 33-34, 83-85, 148-149, 152-153, 190
anorexia nervosa, 64, 112

Bettelheim, Bruno, 154
Bible in counseling, use of, 125-138
bitterness, 34
body language, 75
Built-in User's Manual, 18-25
bulimia, 64, 112-113

challenging persons' behavior patterns, 173-179
Charlie Brown, 39
checklist for learning channels, 217-218
Claypool, John, 136
cohesiveness, group, 197-199
Collins, Gary, 137-138
conflict, mediating, 181-182, 189-192
conflict, resolving, 181-192
conversation focusing, 15-19
Corey, Gerald, 88-89
courage, 38-40
creation (biblical theme), 136

desensitization, 39
disabilities, learning, 107-110
divorce, 68, 174
dyslexia, 108

Egan, Gerard, 179
extramarital affairs, 68, 71
eye contact, 16-17, 22, 47

fear of change, 167-168
fears, overcoming, 27-41, 168-170
feedback, 22, 114, 171, 177, 192
fight or flight (in conflict resolution), 183-185
Fisher, Roger, 188
Francis of Assisi, 15
Frankl, Viktor, 77-78
Freud, Sigmund, 107

gifts, discovering, 104
grief, 53
group counseling, 199-201
grudges, 80

Halverson, Richard C., 191
Holy Spirit, 117, 126

incest, 39, 64
individualizing, 43-48
inductive Bible study, 135
inertia, 167

Jesus Christ, 11-12, 44, 70, 89-90, 126, 154-155, 187-188, 191
Johnson, Samuel, 28
journal writing, 22-23, 171-172
Jung, Carl, 44

Knowles, Malcolm, 110-111

Larson, Bruce, 11-12
logotherapy, 77-78
loneliness, 54-55
love, conditional, 40-41, 54, 64, 147, 149-150

May, Rollo, 121, 168
mentors, 142, 186-187
metaphors in counseling, use of, 145-157
"mum effect," 179

Naisbitt, John, 141
"naming the tune," 57-65, 78
narcissism, 46
networks, counseling, 140-143
Nouwen, Henri J. M., 121

obstacles to change, removing, 161-172

peacemaking, 182-183, 189-191
peak experiences, 156
Peck, M. Scott, 46
Petersen, J. Allan, 71
physical centering, 16-17
psychodrama, 21

questioning, effective, 77-90

reconciliation, 84, 137, 181
rejection, fear of, 31-38, 174-175
relational theology, 136
resistance to change, 159-171, 175
ReST (Renewal-Support-Training) groups, 123, 203-211

Schultz, Charles, 39
self-directed learning, 111-112
Simon, Sid, 102, 167
small groups, leading, 195-201
spiritual growth, 125-134, 145-146, 204
strengths and weaknesses, discerning, 93-106
story-telling in counseling, 150-151, 154
suicide, 102

task competency, 107-112
timing (in counseling), 67-75
topics for conversation, 20-21
touch, 47, 81
Tournier, Paul, 121-122

Ury, William, 188

Wald, Oletta, 135
weakness, accepting, 119-123
Wheat, Ed and Gaye, 135
Wink, Walter, 120-121

Yohn, Rick, 135